THE ABSOLUTE BEGINNERS GUIDE

Working with
Polymer Clay

THE ABSOLUTE BEGINNERS GUIDE

Working with Polymer Clay

Lori Wilkes

KALMBACH BOOKS

Kalmbach Books
21027 Crossroads Circle
Waukesha, Wisconsin 53186
www.Kalmbach.com/Books

Published in 2012

16 15 14 13 12   1 2 3 4 5

Manufactured in the United States of America

ISBN: 978-087116-453-7

EISBN: 978-0-87116-753-8

Editor: Karin Van Voorhees
Art Director: Lisa Bergman
Photographers: James Forbes, William Zuback

Library of Congress Cataloging-in-Publication Data

Wilkes, Lori.

  Working with polymer clay / Lori Wilkes.

  p. : col. ill. ; cm. —(The absolute beginners guide)

  "Everything you need to know to get started"—Cover.

  ISBN: 978-0-87116-453-7

  1. Polymer clay craft—Handbooks, manuals, etc. 2. Jewelry making—Handbooks, manuals, etc. I. Title. II. Title: Polymer clay

  TT297 .W55 2012

  745.594/2

Contents

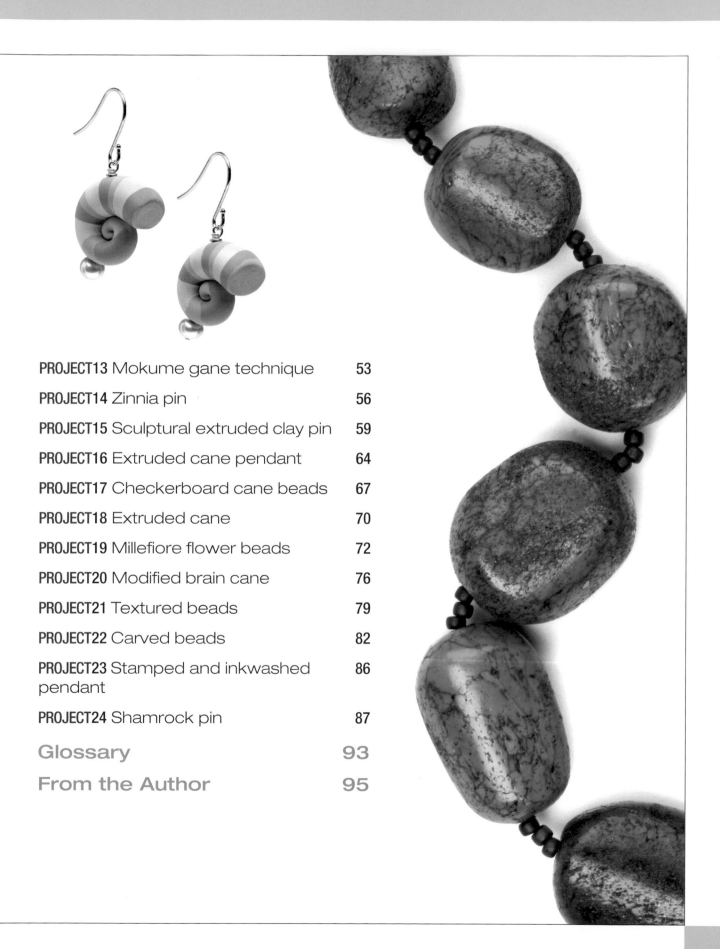

Welcome to the world of polymer clay! I use the term "world" because polymer clay offers incredibly diverse possibilities, especially for jewelry making. From creating realistic faux stones to intricate floral patterns, polymer clay really does have something for everyone. It's also fun, forgiving, and satisfying. I've logged countless hours in my studio and I couldn't do that if I weren't enjoying myself. Mistakes are welcome in this world. Some of my best work has come from a foiled attempt to do something else. And, there is no waste. Polymer clay does not dry out and if stored properly, will be workable for a long time.

Best of all, soon you'll be hearing

"Where did you get that great necklace?" or "Wow, I like your earrings!"

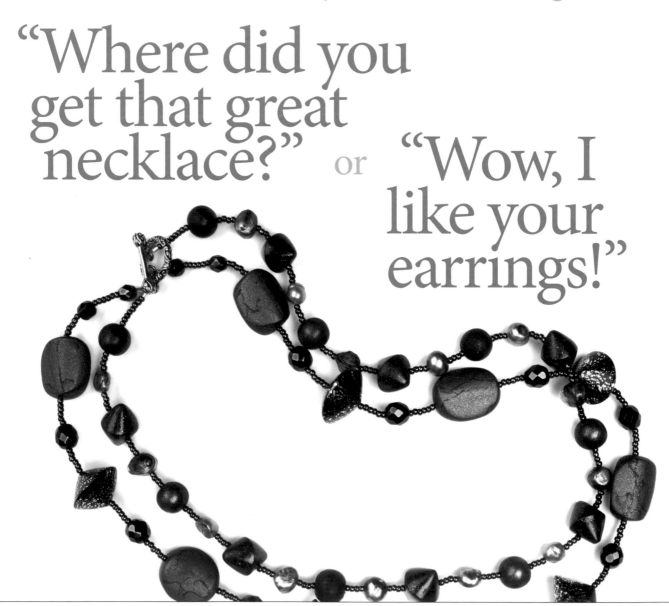

MATERIALS & SUPPLIES

Because this is an absolute beginners guide, my goal is to get you comfortable and creating without a lot of required polymer clay materials, supplies, and tools. Yes, it's quite possible to create fabulous beads using common household items. In fact, you may find yourself scouring your junk drawer and refrigerator to find "tools" to use in your projects! But first, it's important to understand the clay itself.

You'll find that you have many brands to choose from—Sculpey, Premo, Fimo, Kato—which clay is the best? Is there a difference? Some clays, like Fimo Soft and Sculpey, are soft. They are easy to condition and shape with your hands. These clays are great for stamping, texturing, and inclusions. However, softness becomes an issue when building patterns in clay as you'll learn to do with canes. The pattern may smudge or lose its shape. An easy way to understand this is to think about slice-and-bake cookies with patterns inside (such as hearts or shamrocks). The dough must be firm enough to slice and maintain the pretty pattern. If the dough is too warm, it's hard to slice and the pattern becomes distorted. It's the same way with clay. Firm clays such as Kato or Premo hold a pattern, and soft clays have trouble with it. Conditioning firm clays is more work, but it is easily accomplished with a pasta machine.

It's important to note that manufacturers change their formulas occasionally. These days, I do a "press test" at the store. When considering a block of clay, I press the corner to feel how soft it is. The softness or firmness of the clay I buy depends on the project that I'll be making.

Polymer clays come in gorgeous colors. Some even have built in special effects! **Metallic clays** contain mica for a soft metallic luster. **Glitter clays** are fun for making beads: Glitter is suspended throughout the clay so there are no dead spots. (Don't use glitter clays or clays with inclusions for making patterns that need to be sliced, though, because the blade drags the inclusions through the clay and distorts and scratches the pattern.)

Translucent clays are available in many colors. They are not as opaque as the regular solid colors, so they can create depth and transparency. Translucents are also helpful when loosening up clay that is too firm or dry. The translucent acts as an extender medium.

Glow-in-the-dark clays aren't just kid stuff. Use them just like all the other light neutral clays but gain the fringe benefit of being impressive at night.

Liquid polymer clay is used as a sort of polymer "glue" to apply two pieces of clay together (both cured and uncured), or as a curable protective layer for transferred images and foils. Liquid clays are available in several colors.

In addition to clay, there are some other materials and supplies you'll want to have before you begin:

Armor-all release agent: Spray a mold or texture sheet before using to ensure easy release of the clay.

Glues (E-6000, The Ultimate by Crafter's Pick): You'll need a glue that bonds well with the cured clay to attach elements such as pin backs.

Ranger Alcohol Inks: Mix with uncured clay to add color and pattern.

Future acrylic floor polish: Seal the cured piece and provides a nice finish.

Assorted metal leaf (gold, silver, and copper): Sold in paper-thin sheets, these can be layered on or combined with clay for special effects.

Isopropyl alcohol: Use with paper towels to remove all clay residue from your workspace and tools.

Fast Orange hand cleaner: Cleans clay from your hands without drying them out.

Acrylic paints: Add details to cured clay or bring out textures with paint.

TOOLS

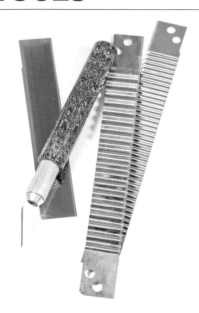

The only non-negotiable must-have tool is a **tissue blade**. Originally made for medical use, these flexible blades are essential for slicing clay. I did not have one of these when I first experimented, and my results reflected it. They're not expensive and you can find them wherever polymer clay is sold. Flexible tissue blades allow you to really bend and cut curves; stiffer blades are great for straight cuts. Wavy ripple blades are also available for creating special cuts. Tissue blades are extremely sharp. The ends are unmarked, so you must pay attention when using these blades. You may want to mark the safe end with paint or a marker.

A **pasta machine** (PM) is also a wonder when working with clay. Though not a necessity, once you use one, you'll never go back to rolling by hand. The machine rolls out consistently thick sheets of clay with the turn of a crank handle. Thickness is adjusted by turning a knob on the machine.

My pasta machine is an Atlas for pasta, but the craft store variety for clay works as well. If you're very lucky, you might find a pasta machine at a yard sale! The pasta machine must have a clamp to attach to a sturdy table.

If you don't have a pasta machine to use for clay, you will need a rolling pin to make sheets of clay. In the polymer clay area of the store, you'll see **clear acrylic rollers** in various sizes. The one I use the most is 8" long. You can use an old rolling pin, but if it is wood,

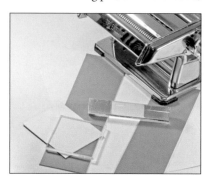

it may leave a texture on the clay. I've used the handle of a craft knife as a roller many times with good results. Acrylic rollers are nice because they are smooth, cheap, and clean up well. To roll out different thicknesses of clay without a PM, stack an equal number of matboard scraps on either side of the clay and roll the clay in the middle. the clay will roll to a thickness equal to the height of the stack.

Now that we've covered the biggies, let's look around the house for other tools that are great for working with clay. : A **3x3" matboard scrap** or similarly sized **sturdy box cover** for rolling or shaping beads. Personally, I like a 3x3" **Plexiglas square** because I can see the bead as I'm shaping it.

Pins and needles in assorted sizes are useful for making marks and holes.

Knitting needles make holes and add textures.

A **craft knife** has many purposes: Use the barrel for rolling, the coupler for texturing, and the blade for cutting.

Plastic straws and **stir sticks** in different sizes make marks or uniform holes in pendants or other items.

Eyeglass screw drivers—both Phillips and standard—are used for marking.

Apply **Pearl-Ex powders** or **paint** to clay with a **paint brush** to enhance the clay's texture.

A **ruler** is useful for measuring clay.

Sandpaper is important for finishing, but can also be used for texturing clay.

Mesh veggie bags add unusual texture (garlic bags are wonderful).

Store open packages of clay in **plastic baggies**—also helpful in keeping colors separate.

Wax paper is used to wrap up canes to keep them dust-free and protect them from sticking to other canes.

Kemper Clay Tools are available in small sets with assorted shapes and sizes. They're nice because they have a little plunger that pushes the clay out of the cutter.

Scrap paper will protecting the tabletop from clay residue.

Use **wire** to stabilize beads as they bake.

Keep a variety of **rubber stamps** on hand for adding texture and patterns to clay.

It is imparative that you commit to a **dedicated oven** for polymer clay. Polymer clay is never to be used in a microwave oven. Toaster and/or craft ovens aren't too expensive and can be also found at yard sales fairly readily. I also recommend having an oven thermometer to check the actual temperature of the oven. Because a toaster oven is small, the beads cure very near to the heat. To prevent bead scorching during oven heat cycles, place a sheet of **aluminum foil** over the beads. The foil can be used over and over again. I line my baking sheet with **parchment paper**. If you bake clay directly on the metal tray, the clay will have a shiny texture when cured. Using parchment paper as a liner prevents this. **Oven timers** are wonderful too. I get so involved in the studio that I could easily forget about beads curing in the basement.

Why a dedicated oven? I say dedicated because once the oven is used for clay, it shouldn't be used for food thereafter. This is a rule that I do not violate—ever. It applies to every tool that I use that originally has a food use. Once it gets used in my clay, it is magically transformed into a clay tool that never returns to the kitchen. This leads me to…

SAFETY

Polymer clay is a very safe medium when used properly. It is rated non-toxic, but it does contain polymers and plasticizers that are better left in the beads and not in the belly. This is why I clean up with a good hand cleaner and never snack while working with clay.

Curing clay also requires attention. Most clays cure in the oven between 265–325°F. When you mix different brands together, choose the lower oven temperature and the longer recommended time. Debbie Jackson, a well-known polymer clay artist, once told me she tells her students, "Longer is stronger." Check the clay package for directions about the bake temperatures and bake times for various thicknesses.

Clay will burn if the oven exceeds the curing temperature. I remember well a very full batch of beads that burned because I did not check the temperature dial on the oven when I put the beads in. Though it didn't smoke much, it did create fumes that I'm sure wouldn't pass a fresh air test. We flushed out the basement air with window fans and all was well—except for all those beads! It turned out that my little one had breezed by the oven and decided to play with the buttons and the temperature dial!

There are times when you might decide that you want to sand or buff a cured piece of clay. Because this will create dust, it's always a good idea to wear a **dust mask** and **eye goggles**.

COLOR

As I mentioned earlier, polymer clays are available in some great colors. As a teacher, I always encourage my students to mix or "customize" their colors to make them their own. Mixing colored polymer clays is just like mixing paints. Remember learning in grade school that yellow and red make orange, and so on? I've been playing with color my whole life, so this is not something that I think consciously about anymore, but for many, it's a wilderness.

The color wheel shows you the primary, secondary, and tertiary colors. Red, yellow, and blue are the primary colors. When two primary colors are combined in equal amounts, the result is a secondary color. Orange, green, and purple are the secondary colors. Tertiary colors result from mixing a primary color with a secondary color. Tertiary colors have hyphenated names telling us the dominant primary involved in the mix. So hearing yellow-green tells you that the dominant color is yellow.

If you have no experience mixing and using colors, I suggest picking up a color wheel at the local art/craft store. They are inexpensive and will be a great help while you are learning about combinations.

Tint and Shades
Basically, adding white will create a tint (pastel) and soften a color. Black darkens colors, making shades. Note: Black will turn yellow into a funky green if used to darken it. To create yellow-gold, add violet instead—keep adding violet to get brown. Violet is the complement to yellow. In fact, mixing any two complementary colors together will result in brown.
Complementary

So what's a complementary color? When you look at a color wheel, the colors that are directly opposite each other are called complements. The complement to green is red, orange is blue, and yellow is violet (purple). When these colors are placed near each other it produces a jarring visual effect. Very often when complements are used together they are toned down.

Analogous colors
Analogous colors are those colors next to each other on the color wheel. If you imagine the color wheel as a pie and you took three slices near each other, you would have three colors with similar "ancestry". They look great together, are much less "active" than complementary colors, and provide low contrast.

Split Complementary
Meeting in the middle, you'll find the split complementary color scheme. Again, looking at the color wheel, find two complements, say, yellow and violet. Look for a step down from the intensity of the complements, but still wanting contrast. Instead of using violet with the yellow, use the adjacent red-violet and blue-violet. It's a fool-proof formula for contrast that won't produce a headache.

Final thoughts on color
If you're stumped for color choices, don't worry. Find a picture in a magazine, a piece of fabric, or even a paint chip in colors that you like from a hardware store. That will help prime your color idea pump. Really follow the color wheel to get the color you want. If the color is

lighter, add white a little at a time until you get there. If the color is darker, add black (or brown if yellow) until the shade is achieved. (Note: Black is very powerful and should be added a smidge at a time.)

Don't forget the metallic clays! They become even more beautiful when mixed with a bit of color. Experiment and see!

Remember this: Jewelry is small, so to make a pattern pop, it must have contrast (lights and darks).

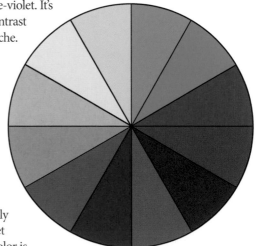

WORKSPACE

In the ideal world, everybody has a studio to work in! I know that's not always possible, so here are some workspace pointers. First, avoid the kitchen. The clay world and the food world must be separated. Don't be afraid of the clay, but unless something says edible on the label, it should not be in the kitchen.

My favorite work surface is a Formica laminate counter or table. (I still work on a piece of scrap paper to help with cleanup and protect the laminate from my blades.) If you don't have a laminate table, a large piece of Plexiglas placed over a protective sheet of paper is a good alternative.

If you're working on a wood table (and I don't recommend this), it's important to protect the tabletop. Work on a piece of scrap paper. Uncured polymer clay will damage wood finishes, including paint, by making them gummy and peely.

The same cautions apply to flooring. Polymer crumbs may end up on the floor causing gummy spots over time. Clay crumbs have left their mark on my painted studio floor, but that just gives me an excuse to paint it again! Be especially careful if your workspace is carpeted. The clay could get ground into the pile with no easy way to remove it. I vacuum my workspace regularly to keep the polymer clay crumbs at bay.

Cleanup

When I clean my area after a polymer clay workout, I wipe down the counter and tools with a paper towel dampened with isopropyl alcohol to dissolve any clay residue. It's important to clean your tools, especially the pasta machine rollers,

with isopropyl alcohol as you work. This prevents color contamination from clay residue.

I use Fast Orange with pumice hand cleaner, because it scrubs my hands and fingers clean without drying out my skin. I use a nailbrush to remove clay from under my nails.

Storage

Polymer clay will remain workable for a long time—if stored properly. Store the clay in a cool, dark place. I store new, unused bricks in plastic drawer organizers. I separate them by color so I can easily see what I have on hand.

Chunks of opened clay get placed in plastic baggies—again separated by color—and stored in a plastic shoe box. Canes get wrapped in plastic wrap and placed in a plastic organizer with square compartments formerly used for nuts and bolts. This keeps dust out and keeps the canes from sticking to each other. I keep all of my clay in a workshop tool cabinet that I adapted for my studio, but clay will store well away from heat and sun.

The warmer the clay gets, the harder the clay will be—it will actually start to cure. This is why, when I purchase clay in the summer, I make buying clay my last stop. Car interiors get mighty hot in the summer, and the heat will actually begin to cure the clay.

This is a simple overview because polymer clay is not complicated. It's really a low-maintenance, waste-free, and fun medium to explore. I often tell students and customers that I'm still at it after all these years because I haven't found the end of the possibilities yet. I suspect I never will.

So, let's dive in! Early projects are easier and teach essential skills. As you progress through the book, you'll add skills that are a little more complex. If you ever get confused along the way, refer to the glossary beginning on page 93.

The Absolute Beginners Guide

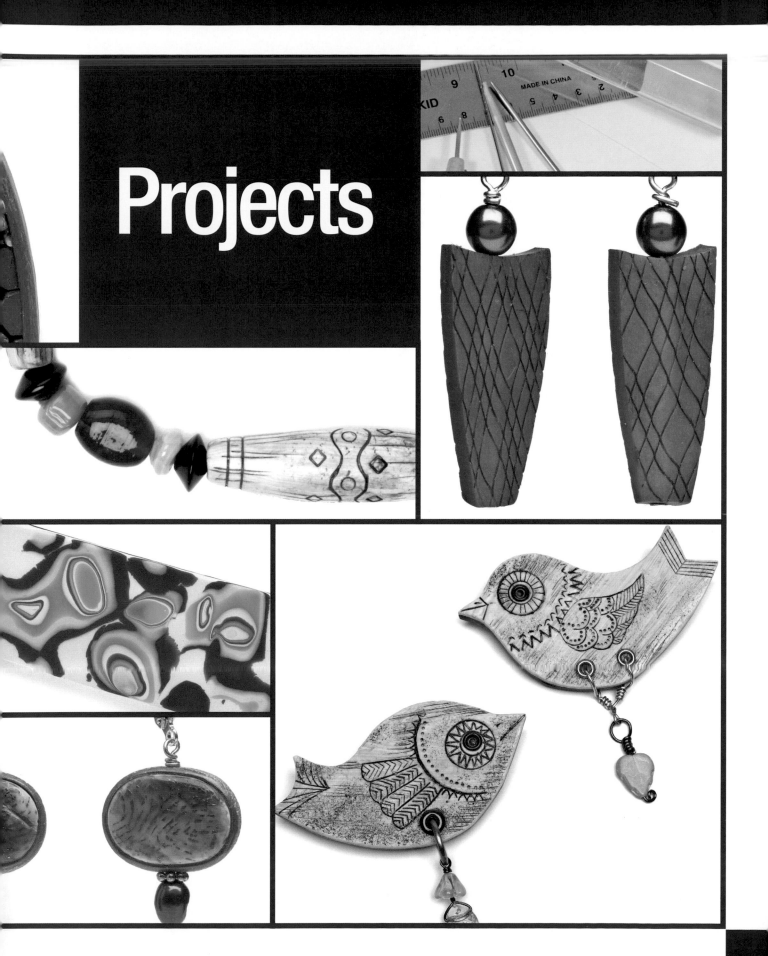

Projects

PROJECT1
Assorted bead shapes

Bead shapes are limited only by your imagination. It is helpful, though, to learn basic techniques in creating and shaping beads that are uniform in shape and size. The following project shows how an analogous color scheme and a variety of basic shapes can work together to make a dynamic necklace.

Finished bead size: ½–¾"

WHAT YOU'LL NEED

Polymer Clay
- ½ brick yellow
- ½ brick purple
- ½ brick green
- ½ brick blue
- ½ brick turquoise blue
- Pinch of white

Tools & Supplies
- Matboard or Plexiglas square
- Ruler
- Tissue blade
- Acrylic roller or brayer
- Skewers
- Dedicated oven
- Foil

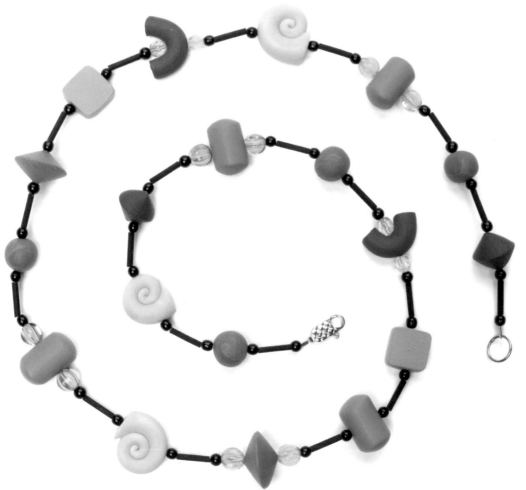

Conditioning clay

Conditioning means to warm up the clay. As clay sits around, its molecules settle into place, making it stiff. In conditioning the clay, the molecules are actually being mixed, much like when you stir paint before using it.

The easiest way to condition clay is to run it through a pasta machine (PM). Take a brick and slice it like cheese for a cracker. Run the slices through the PM. They may go through smoothly, but more often than not, the clay will flake and break up into crumbs. Gather the crumbs and turn the PM dial to the thinnest setting. Run the crumbs through and you'll start to see flatter flakes—keep going. Keep pushing the clay through until it is pliable and smooth. It will get there; it just takes several trips through the PM rollers. If the clay is still crumbly after many trips through the PM, try adding a bit of translucent clay to the crumbs. Translucent clay won't change the color, and it will help the clay become pliable.

Softer clays need less work, but they still should be conditioned with several passes through the PM. The temperature will greatly affect your clay—and conditioning. If the room is warm, the clay will be softer; in fact, if the clay gets too soft, you may need to pop it in the fridge or freezer until it's stiff enough! If the house is cold like mine (yikes!), the "crumbs" scenario becomes more likely. If conditioning without a PM, you will need a pair of pants with pockets, a roller and a sturdy table. The pockets are for warming the clay with your body heat (in the plastic wrap, of course!); the roller is for flattening and rolling the clay, and a sturdy table is important when making just about anything. Knead the clay with your fingers to loosen it up. When it feels like it's becoming flexible, roll it out, fold it, and knead again. However you condition clay, the end result must be pliable, smooth clay ready for action.

Make the beads
1. Condition all clays.

 TIP To make the same size beads, measure the clay. Place the clay log next to a ruler. Select the length that you want and mark the log in equal increments with a needle or a skewer. Then slice the clay into sections.

2. To make the blue beads, roll the clay into a ½" diameter log. Measure and slice in ¼" sections. Roll the sections into rounds by shaping the slices into rough rounds with your fingers and then refining them with the Plexiglas or matboard square. To do this, apply light pressure in a circular motion, holding the square parallel to the table. This takes practice, so keep rolling until you are happy with the shape you made. Skewer the rounds and set aside.

 TIP When skewering, always twist or rifle the skewer while pushing. This will lessen shape distortion and help the skewer pass more easily through the clay.

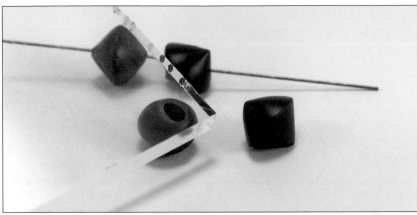

3. For the bicone shape, begin by rolling the unaltered purple clay into a log about ⅜" thick. Place the log along a ruler's edge and measure out several sections ½" long. Cut and roll into rounds as in Step 2.

4. Hold the square at an angle to the table. Continue to roll the clay applying more pressure. You will see the shape change after only a few rolls. Take your time; speed has no effect on the outcome. Skewer and set aside.

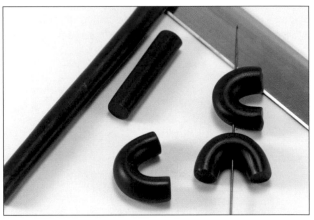

5. Repeat the same process with the lighter purple clay; only make these bicones flatter and wider by applying a bit more pressure while rolling the clay. Skewer and set aside.

6. Roll the blue-violet clay into a log ¼" in diameter. Cut several 1" sections of clay and bend into macaroni shapes. These may be skewered in a number of ways, depending on the necklace design.

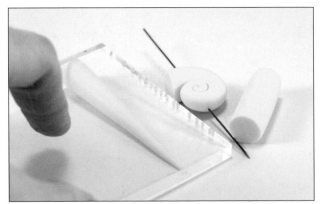

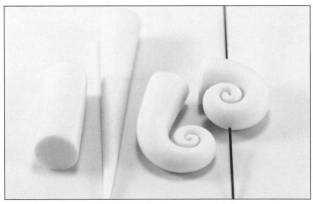

7. Roll the yellow clay into a log ⅜" thick. Cut 2" sections and roll them with the Plexiglas square on an angle so the log becomes tapered on one end.

8. Coil the clay (thinner end first) into a snail shape and skewer as desired.

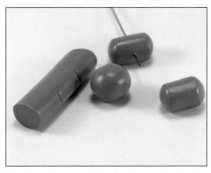

9. Roll the turquoise clay into a log ½" in diameter. Cut several ¾" sections of clay and roll into rounds. To create the cylinder shape, roll the clay into a round, and then roll the round back and forth (not in a circle).

10. To make the green square beads, roll the clay into a log ¾" thick in diameter. Roll over the log with an acrylic roller or a brayer to flatten the top and bottom edges. Turn and repeat to form a square shaped log. Place the clay along a ruler and mark in ¼" increments. Slice the clay. Skewer some of the beads through the middle and some from corner to corner.

11. When all of the beads are made and skewered, it's time to cure them. I call for skewers in most of the projects in this book because they are easy to use and work very well when stringing with beading wire. Preheat the oven to the specified temperature. Place a piece of foil over the beads to cover, and cure in the dedicated oven per manufacturer's instructions.

String as desired.

TIP

Skewers are made to work with a nifty bead curing tray as shown. This tray keeps the beads from touching the pan while curing (which leaves a mark) and allows you to space out the beads however you need. When I began making beads, I didn't have the skewers or the tray. I used lengths of wire crimped over the edge of the oven pan. It worked, but the skewers and tray are a huge improvement. I also use my little oven's baking pan as an under-liner for the bead tray. It seems to make loading the oven easier.

PROJECT2
Sand beads

This is a very simple project that makes surprisingly beautiful beads. You'll need to pick out your favorite color of play sand at your local craft store, or better yet, borrow some from your kids!

TIP

For a bracelet, you will need at least nine ¾" long beads plus spacers and a clasp; for a necklace, make even more beads!

1. Condition clay. Roll the clay into logs. Measure and slice into equal-sized pieces of clay.

2. With some clay from each color, roll three small logs and twist together. Roll to smooth, and slice a few more pieces of clay the same size as before.

3. Roll clay into balls. Pour some navy-colored sand onto a piece of scrap paper.

4. Roll the balls in the sand, covering them well. Roll over the balls to embed the sand. Add more sand, if necessary. Roll into rounds.

TIP Use a square of matboard when rolling in inclusions like sand. The smooth surface of a Plexiglas square will be scratched by the sand.

5. To create pebbles, take the matboard square and roll a clay ball in small circles using light pressure. When the clay is round, stop moving in circles and move back and forth with moderate pressure instead to flatten a bit. The pebbles don't need to be regular in shape. Repeat with the other pieces of clay.

6. Skewer the beads.

TIP

Before stringing, rub the beads gently with your hands to remove any loose sand. String as desired.

7. Cover with foil and cure in a dedicated oven per manufacturer's instructions. Let cool completely.

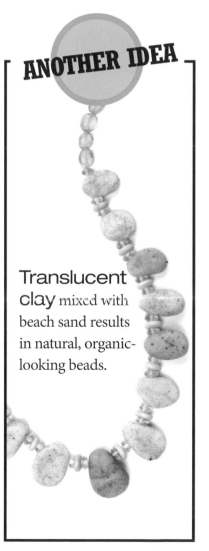

ANOTHER IDEA

Translucent clay mixed with beach sand results in natural, organic-looking beads.

PROJECT3
Textured earrings

This fun project provides practice using household textures and your flexible tissue blade. You'll be amazed at how many items in your home make beautiful textures! This project used a scrap of lace, a bit of a lemon bag, and some leftover ribbon.

Finished length: 1½"

What You'll Need

Polymer Clay
• ¼ brick pink
• ¼ brick yellow
• ¼ brick turquoise

Tools & Supplies
• Flexible tissue blade
• Acrylic roller
• **2** or more long needles or skewers
• Dedicated oven
• Roundnose pliers
• Wire cutters
• Acrylic paint (in contrasting color)
• Paintbrush
• Paper towels
• Pasta machine (PM)
• Foil
• Headpins
• Beads
• Pair of earring wires

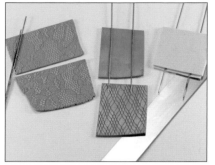

Roll, texture, and shape the clay

1. Condition and mix clay in the desired colors. Roll clay to a ¹⁄₁₆" thickness (thickest setting on PM, or single scrap of matboard on either side of the clay). Select textured fabric (a lace scrap, for example). Place the lace over the clay and gently roll with a round cylinder or acrylic roller.

2. Create a different texture on each sheet of clay.

3. Cut each sheet of clay in half. To make holes for the headpins, take a long needle or skewer that's the same diameter as the headpin. Place the needle on one half-sheet of textured clay. Place a second needle, allowing adequate space between. Place the straight edge of the textured top sheet over the straight edge of the bottom sheet and pins. Gently seal and secure the layers together without disturbing the textures.

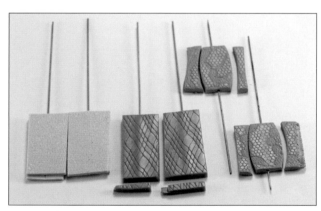

4. Cut in half between the skewers. Shape the earrings by using a flexible tissue blade to create curved edges. Be sure to make two similar-sized earrings.

Finish the beads and enhance the texture

5. Cover with foil. Cure in a dedicated oven per manufacturer's instructions. Let cool.

6. Apply contrasting acrylic paint to the earrings. Wipe off the paint while it is still workable. This will bring out the detail in the textures.

Make earrings

7. Insert headpins and add beads or pearls to the earrings. To finish, use a pair of roundnose pliers to bend the wire headpin into a loop. Twist the wire around the stem and trim excess with wire cutters. Connect the earring to the earring wire.

PROJECT4

Sandpaper beads and necklace

Finished length: 16"

WHAT YOU'LL NEED

Polymer Clay
- ½ brick lime green
- ½ brick dark metallic green
- ¼ brick black

Tools & Supplies
- Ruler
- Tissue blade
- Ripple blade
- Small round cutter
- Small fabric scrap (denim is good)
- 18" beading wire
- 60-grit sandpaper (one piece)
- **2** crimp beads
- **26** 4mm black glass round beads
- Clasp
- Jump ring
- Clay glaze or acrylic floor finish
- Tissue blade
- Roller or pasta machine
- Scrap paper
- Needle tool or skewers
- Dedicated oven

The velvety texture of sandpaper beads is entrancing—and, it's also very easy to create! This project uses the common household helper, sandpaper, and some basic beadmaking techniques to achieve sculptural results.

Make the accent beads

1. Condition clays as usual. Roll the green clays into logs and twist together. Roll the twist to smooth into a log. Twist and roll the log to elongate (and reduce). Fold in half twice and repeat. The stripes will become more and more fine.

2. Roll the log into a long snake about ½" in diameter. Using a ruler, mark the clay in 20 even increments of ⅜" and cut. Roll the slices into round clay balls. Cut the 60-grit sandpaper sheet into fourths and place one of the sandpaper quarters on the work surface. Take a clay ball and place on the sandpaper. Take another quarter of the sandpaper and roll the bead as you would to make a round bead. The bead will take on a velvety texture.

3. Repeat with the remaining beads. Skewer the beads. Cover with foil and cure per manufacturer's instructions.

Make the focal bead

4. Roll the conditioned black clay into a bicone shape. Remember, to make a bicone, begin by rolling the clay into a round with light, circular pressure, keeping the square roller parallel to the tabletop. Once the clay is round, tilt the square and apply more pressure. Take your time rolling; the shape quality is unaffected by speed. Apply increasing pressure to flatten it down, making a button shape of sorts. The goal is a large, round bead that is thicker in the center and thinner at the edges.

5. Using the ripple blade, slice through the center of the black bead.

TIP You may need to roll the clay several times to get a focal bead shape that you like.

6. With the halves together, use a round cutter to slice through the black bead a bit higher than halfway from center.

7. Skewer the black bead halves evenly across the upper half of the bead. Be sure to have the skewer running through the round hole cut in the center. Run the beading wire through the black focal bead halves and one of the textured green beads as shown. This will help you see if the "fit" is right for the green center bead. Adjust the center of the focal bead if necessary with the round cutter. Cure and cool.

8. Lightly sand the focal bead, leaving a small portion untouched for contrast. This will make the black clay look gray.

OPTION When finished, you may opt to rub the clay with a piece of scrap fabric (denim is great for this). This will lightly buff the clay, darkening it a bit while leaving the sandpaper marks intact.

9. To create contrast in textures, apply some clay glaze or acrylic floor finish to the inside edges of the black bead.

Let dry and string as shown on page 22.

ANOTHER IDEA

To make these velvety looking earrings, measure out two equal size pieces of clay and roll into rounds between two sheets of 60-grit sandpaper.

PROJECT5
Faux lapis

Lapis is a very elegant stone. It's subtle, yet substantial. By following the next few steps, you will be able to create your own beautiful "lapis" stone.

Finished length: 17"

WHAT YOU'LL NEED

Polymer Clay
- ½ brick ultramarine
- ½ brick navy blue
- ¼ brick translucent
- scrap clay

Tools & Supplies
- Waxed paper
- Gold leaf booklet
- Gold Pearl-Ex dust
- Paintbrush
- Scrap paper
- Roller or pasta machine
- Kitchen grater
- Clay glaze or acrylic floor finish
- Dedicated oven

Faux lapis cane
1. Condition clays as usual. Grate the blue clays on the large-hole side of the grater. They will be mixed together, so don't worry about keeping them separate.

2. Next, roll out a very thin sheet of the translucent clay. If you have a pasta machine, use the thinnest setting; if not, roll out the clay as thin as possible with the acrylic roller between two sheets of waxed paper. Leaving the gold leaf on the tissue paper page, carefully place the translucent clay over the gold leaf sheet and remove from booklet. Turn clay over and gently smooth the leaf down with your fingertip.

3. Starting on one end, roll the gold leaf clay sheet tightly into a log and cut off a ½" section. (Reserve the remaining log for Project #12.)

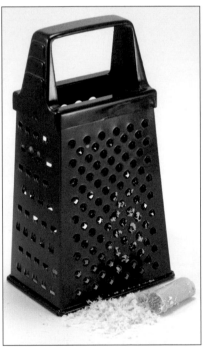

4. Grate the section on the fine side of the grater. This step adds tiny gold flecks to the lapis "stone."

5. Use a paintbrush to lightly dust the blue clay with some gold Pearl-Ex.

6. Toss all of the grated clays together. Chop through the clay pile with a tissue blade several times.

7. Gather up the clay crumbs and roll into a 3" log. Keep rolling to elongate (or reduce) until the log is 12" long.

8. Cut into fourths. Combine the fourths and roll to smooth. You have just made a faux lapis cane!

There's an added benefit to translucent clay: Use it to revive old, hardened bricks of clay that are nearly unusable. Chop the stiff colored clay into chunks and pop it into an old food processor or coffee bean grinder. Process the clay into crumbs, add a few chunks of translucent clay, and process the clays together for a few seconds. Remove the lid and squeeze some clay in your hand to see if it holds together. If it's still too crumbly, add more translucent clay and process again.

Making a 17" Necklace

19 polymer clay faux lapis round beads
7 wooden square beads with round center cut
22 11º gold seed beads
2 crimp tubes
clasp
jump ring
flexible beading wire

String necklace as shown on page 25. Adjust the fit by adding or removing beads.

Make the Beads

9. This particular necklace requires some planning and measuring because of the interior space of the wooden beads. You will need to figure out how much clay you'll need to make the beads. You can do this by simply rolling up a round bead using scrap clay and checking the fit. When you find the right amount, roll the bead into a cylinder with flat ends. Roll out a scrap clay log to the same diameter as the cylinder. Now measure the length of the cylinder and mark this length on the scrap clay log and slice into sections. My clay log is ½" in diameter and 8" long. Mark and cut the roll into ¼" increments.

I used red clay here as a demo, but always try to use a similar color for your "under" bead. This way, if the cane slice doesn't quite cover, it's less visible.

10. Make thin slices from the lapis log and cover the scrap clay beads.

11. Recheck the size of the beads to insure that they fit into the space. Adjust as necessary. Roll until smooth with the matboard or Plexiglas square. Check to make sure the scrap clay underneath is covered. Patch, if necessary, with a bit of the lapis. Repeat with the remaining clay rounds. Skewer the beads. Cure in a dedicated oven per manufacturer's instructions. Let cool.

12. Apply two thin coats of acrylic floor finish or clay glaze for shine.

ANOTHER IDEA

This necklace features

a cabochon. To make it, cover a larger ball of scrap clay with slices of lapis cane. Roll the ball to smooth, and flatten it into a domed oval. Always be sure that your cabochon is flush to the bottom edge. This will help when adding beads around the shape during finishing.

PROJECT6
Faux turquoise

Turquoise comes in many different colors so use your imagination and mix up your favorite shade! To make a more realistic necklace, make a few canes with slightly different tones.

TIP

The most successful turquoise necklaces have very subtle color variations. When mixing in color, use a light hand.

Here some color mixing possibilities:

Green turquoise = 1 brick turquoise + ⅛ brick (yellow-green).

For a lighter green, add a bit of white.

Blue turquoise = Use straight out of the package. Lighten with a bit of white.

2. Keeping the colors separate, lightly coat the turquoise clays with either burnt umber or raw sienna-colored acrylic paint. This can be done with a brush, but I usually end up using my fingers to coat the clay properly. Let dry completely. Spread out the clay crumbs on some scrap paper to facilitate drying.

3. Toss in the translucent clay crumbs. If you decide to add a (very) few copper clay crumbs, now is the time to do so. Lightly brush on some silver Pearl-Ex here and there to the clay pile. Toss the crumbs around again.

1. Condition clays as usual. Thoroughly mix turquoise clay with other colors as desired. Grate the mixed clay on the large-hole side of the grater. (Note: I grated three different tones of turquoise clay for three different canes.) Grate the translucent clay on the fine side of the grater. Set aside.

4. Gather the clay crumbs into your hand and squeeze together, forming a lumpy log. Roll the log to help bind the clay. There can be some bumps; it doesn't have to be perfectly smooth.

5. Slice the cane with the tissue blade. You will see a wonderful "stone" matrix in the clay. Set aside.

6. Condition some scrap clay and make random-sized balls to be covered with the turquoise cane. Make thin slices of the turquoise cane and cover the scrap clay completely.

NOTE This is the point where you decide on the overall look of the necklace. If you want to make a bold statement, make bigger beads!

7. Roll the ball smooth. Repeat with the rest of the clay.

8. To add more texture, drop some of the beads into the beach sand to lightly coat. For other beads, just add the sand here and there. This will make the finished beads look more natural.

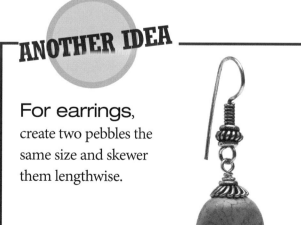

9. On some scrap paper, roll the beads (using a matboard square; the sand will scratch Plexiglas) into pebbles and embed the sand. Skewer the beads and cure in a dedicated oven per manufacturer's instructions. Cool completely.

10. Add a coat of raw sienna paint to the beads. Wipe off the excess paint with a slightly damp paper towel. (This ages and mellows the beads.) Let dry.

11. For a satin finish, add one coat of acrylic floor finish or clay glaze to the beads.

ANOTHER IDEA

For earrings, create two pebbles the same size and skewer them lengthwise.

PROJECT7
Faux bone

This technique yields realistic, natural-looking bone. It's also a great exercise in adding "home-found" textures! Scour your junk drawers for anything that will make interesting marks on the clay. Bristle brushes, a screwdriver, straws … they all make great textures. This project makes enough faux bone clay for two pins.

Finished length: 2½"

WHAT YOU'LL NEED

Polymer Clay
- ½ brick white
- ⅛ brick tan
- ⅛ brick translucent
- ¼ brick black
- ¼ brick any color

Tools & Supplies
- Roller or pasta machine
- Scrap paper
- Pencil
- Scissors
- Tissue blade
- Craft knife
- Burnt umber acrylic paint
- E-6000 adhesive
- Pin back
- Beads
- Wire
- Grommets
- 400-grit sandpaper or Dremel drill fitted with a felt disk
- Dedicated oven
- Various "home-found" tools: pins, an eyeglass screwdriver, a bristle brush, straws, vegetable netting

Bone Cane

1. Condition the clay. Roll the white clay into a 4" log. Roll the tan clay into two 4" logs. Roll the translucent clay into a 4" log. In alternating fashion, attach the tan and translucent clays to the white clay log.

2. Roll to smooth. Twist the log and roll until log is 12" long.

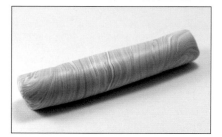

3. Cut log into fourths and stack them back together to make a shorter log. Gently press the logs together and roll and twist again into a log.

4. Repeat two more times and roll the cane to 6" in length. You have made your first bone cane!

Make the pin

5. Cut 3" from the bone cane, setting aside the remainder for another use. With the roller, flatten out the section of cane so that a 3" width is maintained. Continue to roll the clay to ¹⁄₁₆" thick (or the thickest setting on the pasta machine) and approximately 6½" in length.

6. Draw a paper template of the pins you would like to make. (Note: Be sure that the size of the pins will accommodate the pin-back that you have.) Cut out the paper template(s) and place onto the sheet of faux bone clay.

7. Cut the clay around the template with a flexible tissue blade and/or a craft knife.

8. Place the shape on a conditioned piece of colored clay ⅛" thick. Add "bone textures" to the clay by jabbing the sheet randomly with a stiff bristle brush. Also, make random, light-pressure strikes with a needle on the clay, running with the grain of the bone stripes. Add details and patterns to the bird or fish with your "home-found" tools. Cut it out as before.

TIP You may also run the netting and the clay through the PM. Simply turn the thickness setting up one click, place the netting over the sheet, and run it through!

9. Add grommets for the eyes by pressing them into the clay. Add gromets for bead dangles, if desired. Clear away any clay from the holes.

10. Next, roll out a thin sheet of the black clay (second-thinnest setting on the pasta machine). Lay a piece of vegetable netting on the clay and roll over the top of it, impressing the net onto the surface. Peel the netting from the clay.

11. Turn the textured black clay over and place the pin on top of the clay. Gently roll or tap over the clay to adhere the layers. Cut around the shape (for the backing).

12. Set the prongs of the pin-back into the clay and remove. Cure flat on a baking sheet lined with parchment paper as directed and let cool.

13. Apply a thin layer of the Burnt Umber acrylic paint to the surface of the clay. Rub the paint into the details with your fingertip.

14. With a dampened paper towel, remove the excess paint and let dry.

15. Sand with 400-grit sandpaper to smooth. Or, use a Dremel drill with a felt buffing disk.

16. Add bead dangles as desired. Apply E-6000 glue to the pin back and place it into the prong holes on the back of the cured clay pin. Let the adhesive dry.

ANOTHER IDEA

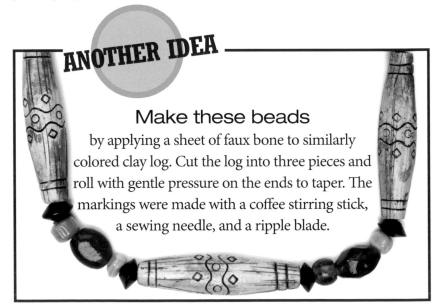

Make these beads

by applying a sheet of faux bone to similarly colored clay log. Cut the log into three pieces and roll with gentle pressure on the ends to taper. The markings were made with a coffee stirring stick, a sewing needle, and a ripple blade.

PROJECT8
Faux jade

Finished length: 17"

What You'll Need

Polymer Clay
- ¼ brick translucent
- ⅛ brick translucent blue
- ⅛ brick green
- Light-colored scrap clay

Tools & Supplies
- Kitchen grater
- Matboard roller
- Scrap paper
- Paint mixing tray
- Tissue blade
- 400-grit sandpaper
- 600-grit sandpaper
- Acrylic floor finish
- Paintbrush
- E-6000
- Beading substrate (Lacy's Stiff Stuff)
- Iridescent glitter (Arnold Grummer's Flakes)
- Meadow and Stream Ranger alcohol inks
- Dedicated oven

One of the greatest things about polymer clay is the ability to create "stones" that are the exact color that I am looking for! Jade is one of those stones that you can make just the way you want it. If you prefer dark jade, boost the color. If you want a softer tone, simply decrease the amount of colored clay in the mix.

2. In the meantime, mix and condition the remaining translucent, blue, and green clays together. Cut one fourth of the clay away and grate it on the large-hole side of the grater.

3. With a brush, lightly dab a mixture of Meadow and Stream alcohol inks onto the grated chunks of clay. Let dry. This will add natural-looking variegation to the cabochons.

1. Condition clays. Take ⅛ brick translucent clay and grate it on the fine side of the grater. Add a pinch of the iridescent glitter and toss together. Cure the crumb-glitter mixture in the dedicated oven and cool completely.

4. Add the cured translucent/glitter clay crumbs to the remaining jade green clay. Mix well and then grate on the large-hole side of the grater.

5. Toss the two grated clays together to mix. Make sure that the inked clay chunks are dispersed evenly throughout.

6. Gather the clay together to form a log.

7. With the matboard, roll clay to make a smooth cane.

TIP

A cabochon (cab) is a ball that has been flattened and formed into a convex shape. You can replicate a cabochon shape by tracing around an existing cab and using the tracing as a guide when shaping and sizing your cab. Remember to make the bottom edge as flat as possible. This will make beading around the cabochon easier, yielding better results.

8. Take thin slices of the cane and cover a light-colored ball of conditioned scrap clay. Roll the covered ball with the matboard to smooth. Shape the ball into desired cabochon shape.

9. If you'd like to boost the color, wet a brush with alcohol and place one drop each of the Meadow and Stream alcohol inks into different ends of a mixing tray. Pick up some of each color without mixing together. Random is better. Wash the ink over the cabochon and let dry.

Finishing
10. Cure and cool as directed.

11. Wet sand the cabochon with 400-grit wet/dry sandpaper to smooth out any bumps. Repeat with the 600-grit paper.

TIP Sanding is VERY important! If you neglect this step, your cabochon will not live up to its potential! Add two or three coats of acrylic floor finish and let dry between coats. Glue the cabochon to the beading substrate with an adhesive such as E-6000 and let cure.

ANOTHER IDEA

This simple pendant is just a large, faux jade-covered ball rolled round and then back and forth to elongate slightly. I wrapped hemp cord around the bead several times and tucked the ends into the uncured clay. I finished the piece with a fine wire wrap that included a freshwater pearl.

PROJECT9
Bollywood beads

Finished length: 18"

What You'll Need

Polymer Clay
- 2 clay bricks fuchsia
- ½ clay brick gold
- ⅛ brick green
- ¼ brick orange
- Scrap clay

Tools & Supplies
- Pearl-Ex powder, brilliant gold
- Small paintbrush
- Gold leaf (half sheet)
- Tissue blade
- Ruler
- Marxit tool
- Matboard
- Acrylic roller or pasta machine
- Scrap paper
- Dedicated oven
- Acrylic floor finish
- Isopropyl alcohol

This necklace is all about adding metallics to your beads for a little bling and a lot of impact. The fuchsia beads use cracked foil, the orange beads are dusted with gold Pearl-Ex and the green/gold beads are made with metallic clay.

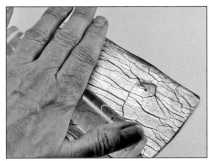

Cracked foil technique

1. Condition all clays. Cut the fuchsia clay in half and roll out a sheet approximately 3x5½" on the thickest setting of your pasta machine. Carefully place the clay onto the gold leaf. It's important to eyeball this closely because once the clay is on the foil, it will be stuck there.

2. Turn the clay over and gently smooth the foil down with your fingertips to secure and flatten blisters. Patch bare spots with bits of extra leaf. Smooth.

3. Roll over the clay with an acrylic roller, or run the sheet through the pasta machine on the second-thickest setting. You will notice the leaf fracturing. Continue to roll until clay is 1/32" thick (the second-thinnest setting on the pasta machine.)

Cracked foil bicones

4. Roll out some scrap clay into a ½" diameter log. Cut five 1"sections and two ½" sections. Roll sections into rounds. Cover the rounds with the fuchsia sheet of fractured gold leaf. To do this, tear off pieces as needed in order to completely cover the scrap clay. If you don't have scrap clay, use fuchsia-colored clay as your under-bead. (Be careful not to trap any air under the sheet.) Repeat with the other rounds.

5. On a piece of scrap paper, roll the rounds to smooth down the clay using a square piece of matboard or Plexiglas. Begin to make a bicone (pointy on the top and bottom) with the matboard or Plexiglas. Remember, to do this, simply move the matboard in a circle and begin to apply more pressure. I made flatter bicones by rolling a bit longer than I do for a balanced bicone. Repeat with the other covered beads.

The foil leaf will fracture differently when rolled in one direction versus rolling in both directions. The leaf will also fracture differently with stiff or soft clays. Experiment to see the different looks.

Metal leaf comes in three colors: gold, silver, and copper. It's difficult to handle because it's incredibly fragile. To avoid waste, don't touch it. Leave it on the tissue paper it comes on until you're ready to use it.

6. Skewer the flattened bicones from side to side.

Fuchsia bicones

7. Roll a ½" diameter log of fuchsia clay and cut it into four ½" sections. Roll the sections into four balanced bicones (even in width and length). Skewer from tip to tip.

Orange rounds

8. For the orange beads, roll out a ¼" diameter log. Measure and cut six even sections about ¼" long. Roll into rounds and skewer. In this photo, I'm showing the Marxit tool. This makes measuring equal amounts of clay a snap. Just roll out a clay log and impress the clay with your choice of increments.

NOTE Be sure to wipe your Marxit tool with isopropyl alcohol after each use. The manufacturer used a material that will soften and get gooey if clay is left stuck to it over time.

9. Skewer the orange beads and with a soft brush, apply some Pearl-Ex Brilliant Gold. Set aside.

Green/gold metallic pebbles

10. To make the green/gold pebbles, mix ½ brick of gold clay with ¼ brick of green clay. Roll together into a thin sheet. Roll the scrap clay into a log ½" in diameter. Slice nine ½" sections and roll into rounds. Cover the scrap rounds with the green/gold clay.

11. Roll the bead to smooth. Check the covered round for air blisters. If you find one, take a tissue blade and slice under one side of it. Re-roll the clay to smooth and mend the slice mark.

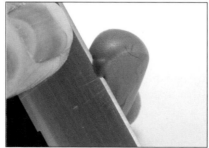

12. Roll into a round and then roll into a pebble. Skewer from end to end.

Finishing

13. Cure all of the beads in a dedicated oven per manufacturer's instructions. Let cool completely.

14. Apply two coats of acrylic floor finish to the foil beads. This will add shine and protect the gold leaf.

NOTE This is a necessary step when working with leaf. Otherwise, the foil will wear off eventually.

15. String as shown on page 38. My necklace is double-stranded. The inside strand is 16" and the outside strand is 18".

ANOTHER IDEA

For this necklace,

I used all of the same shapes and techniques from the Bollywood bead project, but in an analogous color scheme of blues and violet and fractured silver leaf.

PROJECT10
Marbleized clay stretch bracelet

Easy and fun, this bracelet shows how stripes can be manipulated to form beautiful random patterns in clay. I've also added a stripe to the sides of the tile beads for extra detail.

What You'll Need

Finished length: 9"

Polymer Clay
• Several colors of polymer clay, ¼ brick each

Tools & Supplies
• Ruler or any straight edge
• Knitting needle or clay tool
• Acrylic roller or pasta machine
• Tissue blade
• Elastic cord
• Spacer beads
• Oval cutter (Makin's Clay)
• Skewers
• Small hand drill
• Dedicated oven

Marbleize
1. Gather up several clays in colors that look nice together. Condition.

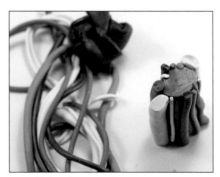

2. Roll the clays into logs in varying thicknesses. Place the colored clays next to each other. I made several marbled patterns for my bracelet. This is a good excuse to practice this new technique and it will produce a more interesting bracelet.

3. Roll lightly to adhere the clays together. Twist both ends of the log in opposite directions. The twisting will naturally make the log longer. You want to avoid this, so after a few twists, gently roll the ends of the clay toward the center to shorten. This will make the log chubby. This is good.

4. Keep twisting and shortening until the stripes on the log go from diagonal to vertical.

5. Press the log a bit to flatten it, using an acrylic roller. Run the sheet through the pasta machine on the thickest setting (1/16").

TIP

To create a chevron pattern in the clay, alternate the direction that you draw the tip across the clay.

6. Take a knitting needle or clay tool and draw the tip across the stripes. The little drag marks are the beginnings of the marbleized pattern. Continue marking as desired.

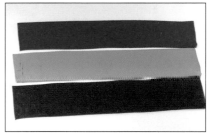

7. Once the marbleizing is finished, gently roll over the clay with a piece of waxed paper on top or run it through the pasta machine on the second-thickest setting to smooth the ridges made by the knitting needle.

8. Use a 1½x1⅛" oval cutter to cut out ovals from the sheets of clay. You'll need between seven and eight ovals for a bracelet, depending on wrist size. Set ovals aside.

9. Roll out three sheets of clay in colors that relate to the colors of the ovals. The sheets should be 1¾x9" and around 1/16" thick.

NOTE Rolling the clay across the drawn lines in the pattern will spread it out. Rolling with the lines will lengthen the pattern.

10. Carefully place the marbleized ovals on top of one of the sheets (blue). Set aside.

11. Texture one of the sheets (the brown backing) with a lemon bag or some other "found" household texture. Set aside.

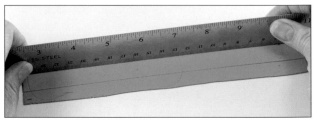

12. Lightly mark the shape of the ovals on both ends of the middle green sheet with the oval cutter. Take a ruler or straight edge and make two lines across the clay about ³⁄₁₆" away from the **center** of the oval. These lines will form the channels for the elastic cord. Make sure the impression left by the ruler is deep enough to accommodate the elastic cord, but does not cut all the way through the clay.

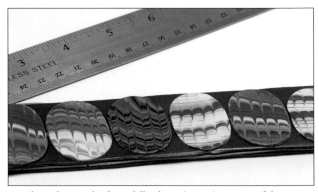

13. Place the marked, middle sheet (green) on top of the untextured side of the brown backing sheet, lining up the edges without trapping air. Place the top oval sheet (blue) over the other two sheets.

This is a fun and easy technique. To make this necklace, I marbled some striped purple clay, cut out rounds with a cookie cutter, and applied a thin sheet of clay to the edges to finish.

14. Use the oval cutter to cut the ovals from the clay.

15. Carefully place skewers through the channels made by the ruler. You may leave these in while curing if you wish. Cure in a dedicated oven per manufacturer's instructions. Let cool completely.

16. Take a stiff tissue blade and cut about ⅛" from the backside of the beads on an angle to form a beveled edge. Trim carefully! Once it's cut, can't be put back. The beveled edge makes the bracelet fit better on the wrist.

Finishing

17. Sand the edges and the top with 400-grit wet/dry sandpaper (or buff lightly with a Dremel drill fitted with a felt disk).

Lay out the bracelet and spacer beads.

18. String elastic cord through the tile beads with small spacer beads in between. If the tile bead holes are too small for the elastic, simply enlarge the holes with a small hand drill. On the bracelet end, make sure that the bead holes are just large enough to counter-sink the knot tied in the elastic.

19. Tie the cord ends with a surgeon's knot. Set the knot with super glue, clip the excess elastic, and tuck the knot into the hole.

TIP Add shine with acrylic floor finish.

PROJECT 11
All about stripes

This project might look complicated, but it really isn't. It's all about stripes made by layering sheets of clay and then rolling, stacking, and cutting in different directions—yielding very different results.

Finished length: 18"

What You'll Need

Polymer Clay
- 2 bricks turquoise
- ½ brick turquoise and ½ brick white mixed to make light turquoise
- Liquid polymer clay

Tools & Supplies
- Paintbrush
- Tissue blade
- Acrylic roller or pasta machine
- Scrap paper
- Ruler
- Dedicated oven
- Needle tool
- Skewers
- 400-grit wet/dry sandpaper

TIP

To reduce or elongate a square cane, you must alternate between twisting and rolling over each side of the cane with a roller or a brayer.

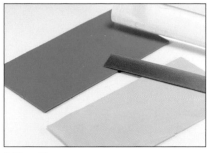

Jelly roll

1. Condition clays. Roll both clays into 1/16"-thick rectangular sheets (or the thickest setting on the PM).

2. Cut the light turquoise sheet 1/8" shorter than the other and place it on top of the turquoise sheet, matching one end. Lightly flatten the matched end and begin to tightly roll the clay into a log.

3. When finished, roll over the edge of the turquoise clay to cover the light turquoise clay.

Congratulations! You've just made a jelly roll cane.

Complex jelly roll cane

4. Roll the jelly roll cane until it is 1/2" in diameter. Cut off 2½" inches and set the rest of the jelly roll aside.

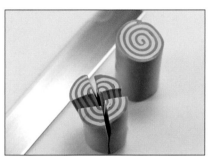

5. Stand the cut section on end. With a tissue blade, cut through the middle of the cane, creating two halves. Then cut these into quarters.

6. Roll to reduce the remaining jelly roll cane to 3/8" diameter. Cut a 2½" section. Place the cut quarters along the side of the jelly roll with the points facing out. This will make a square. Gently press the cane together and reduce the cane until it is four times the length (approximately 10").

7. Trim the ends. Cut the cane in half and then in half again to make four equal sections. Put the four pieces back together, matching the pattern on each end of the cane. Gently press the cane together and roll over it with an acrylic roller.

Stripes

8. Roll out a 4x6" rectangle of clay in each color. Place the light turquoise on top of the turquoise clay. Cut the length of the rectangle in half so that it's 4x3".

9. Restack the clay. Cut in half again on the long side to create a sheet 2x3". Restack and cut once more, but this time cut along the 2" width, yielding a rectangle 1x3". Restack the clay and trim the edges.

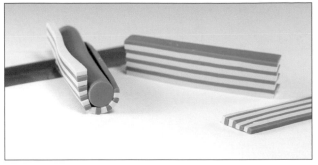

Make a stripe-covered cane

10. Roll a log of the turquoise clay to ½" diameter and 3" long. Make three thin slices of the striped cane (on the long side). Place the slices carefully along the length of the turquoise log matching the pattern. Trim if necessary.

ANOTHER IDEA

There are SO many great ways to use stripes! For these earrings, I made some stripes with warm grays, shaped the clay into snails, skewered, and added pearls.

11. Roll to smooth edges down. The diameter should be ⅜".

NOTE This cane will be used to make the round pattern slices, striped beads and snail-shaped beads.

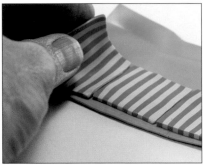

Make striped edges

12. Roll out a thin sheet of turquoise clay at least three inches long. Make several thin slices of the striped cane and place side by side, matching the stripe edges on the clay sheet.

13. Gently roll with the stripes to smooth and elongate them or run the sheet (lengthwise) through the PM on the number three setting. Set aside.

Additional Beads

Striped beads

Take the remaining stripe log and cut two ⅜" sections. Stand the sections on end and gently flatten them with end of roller, forming chubby disks.

Cut a ½" section of cane and roll to reduce it to ¼" diameter. Trim the ends and cut into quarters again; flatten a bit with the end of the roller. Skewer through the middle. Cure as directed

Snail beads

Cut two ¾" sections of the stripe cane. Roll one end down to ⅛" and twist the cane a bit. Roll the clay up, starting with the small end. You will make a snail shape. Repeat with the other bead. Skewer. Cure as directed. Let cool and string necklace as desired.

See Project 1 for more on this technique.

Make a necklace

14. Roll out six turquoise and two light turquoise-colored beads. You may opt to make them all the same size or have graduated sizes. Cut several thin slices of the jelly roll cane and place randomly over the other two turquoise and light turquoise beads. Repeat with thin slices from the striped covered cane and place randomly over four of the turquoise beads.

15. Roll each bead to smooth down the cane slices and make into rounds.

16. Using the end of an acrylic roller, gently flatten the rounds. Skewer and set aside.

Complex jelly roll square beads
17. Roll out a sheet of turquoise clay 1x3¼". Make three thin slices of the complex jelly roll cane and place each on top of the slab of clay. Be sure to turn the cane after each slice to prevent distortion. Cut the slab apart between the cane slices to yield three beads.

18. Turn the beads over and place three more slices of the cane on the blank side. Trim the clay slab, if necessary.

19. Skewer corner to corner or through the middle.

20. Cure the beads in a dedicated oven per manufacturer's instructions. Let cool completely.

21. Measure the height and perimeter of the square beads, and cut strips of the striped sheet long enough to wrap around the sides. Brush a small amount of liquid polymer clay to the cured edges to help bond the raw clay to the cured. Apply the strips to the edge, matching the ends and smoothing the seams with a needle tool. Clear the skewer holes and trim excess clay with a tissue blade.

Cure the beads in a dedicated oven per manufacturer's instructions and let cool. Sand the square beads to smooth edges with 400-grit wet/dry sandpaper.

PROJECT12
Transparent jelly roll cane earrings

This project introduces you to the beauty of ink washes on clay. We're kicking it up a notch by adding a translucent clay overlay. The end result is a dreamy, watercolor effect with delicate gold swirls suspended over the surface.

Finished length: 1"

What You'll Need

Polymer Clay
- ¼ brick transparent clay
- ¼ brick gold clay
- Liquid polymer clay

Tools & Supplies
- Gold leaf sheet
- Scrap paper
- Acrylic roller or pasta machine
- Needle tool
- Assorted alcohol inks
- Isopropyl alcohol
- Tissue blade
- Small oval cutter
- 600-grit wet/dry sandpaper
- 60-grit sandpaper
- Skewers
- Dedicated oven
- Dremel drill fitted with felt disk for buffing
- Plastic wrap

1. Make a very thin 6x6" sheet of transparent clay (use the thinnest setting on the PM). Apply a sheet of gold leaf to the clay.

2. Roll up tightly and expel air.

NOTE In Project #5, Faux Lapis, we made this transparent jelly roll cane. Look for it in your stash.

3. Slice into the cane on an acute angle and make very thin slices.

TIP The thinner the slices, the better the outcome. Practice!

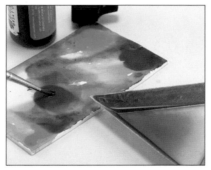

4. Roll out a sheet of white clay ⅟₁₆" or the thickest setting on the PM. Brush or spritz the clay lightly with isopropyl alcohol. Add a few drops of alcohol inks to the surface in desired colors. Let dry.

5. Randomly place the thin cane slices over the clay to cover the ink.

6. Roll with an acrylic roller to smooth the slices and thin the sheet, or run it through the PM, gradually thinning the sheet to the second-thinnest setting.

7. Place the sheet onto another sheet of light-colored clay ⅟₁₆" thick, being careful to avoid trapping air.

8. Place a piece of plastic wrap over the clay and punch out at least four ovals with the small cutter. (As you can see, I made many more!) Cutting through plastic wrap creates a rounded edge.

9. Pair the cut-outs as fronts and backs, (you can make the earrings reversible by using different colors) and gently press together without distorting, Skewer with a needle tool. Cure in a dedicated oven per manufacturer's instructions. Sand the colored surface of the cooled beads with 600-grit wet/dry sandpaper. Sand the edges smooth with 60-grit sandpaper.

ANOTHER IDEA

10. Roll out a thin, rectangular sheet of gold clay (second-thinnest setting on the PM). Texture the clay with 60-grit sandpaper and trim the edges. Cut long strips of clay that are approximately ⅛" wide to cover the seam.

11. Starting in the center, apply the strip of gold clay around the bead.

 TIP When applying raw clay to cured, smear some liquid polymer clay over the area to help bind the clays.

12. Trim the strip so that the ends meet. Gently roll over the top of the strip with a needle tool to secure it. Heal the strip's seam by carefully smoothing over it with a needle tool. Retexture with the sandpaper if necessary. Smooth the edges with your fingertip by gently stroking over the edge of the clay.

Skewer and cure as directed. Let cool. Apply two or three coats of acrylic floor finish to the colored clay, leaving the band matte. Finish as shown.

I rolled the jelly roll cane slices over a translucent clay ball and shaped it into a cabochon. Remember to sand the cabochon with 600-grit sandpaper.

PROJECT 13
Mokume gane technique

The centuries-old mokume gane technique comes to us from Japanese metal artisans. It is a type of metal lamination that yields a very organic, burl-wood finish. Fortunately for us, it is easily adapted to clay.

Finished barrette length: 4¼"
What You'll Need

Polymer Clay
- ½ brick white
- ½ brick fuchsia
- ½ brick turquoise blue
- ½ brick yellow

Tools & Supplies
- Pasta Machine
- Flexible Tissue blade
- Scrap paper
- Paper template
- Waxed paper
- Aluminum foil
- E-6000 adhesive
- Dedicated oven
- 6–12mm glass beads in various shapes
- Barrette blank

1. Begin by collecting several different colors of clay that look good together. This technique works best with contrasting colors and values of clay. I chose four different colors. Condition the clays as usual. Roll clays into ⅟₁₆" thick sheets. My clay sheets are 2¾x2". Trim as necessary and stack the clays in a high-contrast order. Reserve extra clay for later on. Roll the stack lengthwise until it nearly doubles in size.

2. Cut in half again and restack the clay. Trim edges.

3. Re-roll the stack lengthwise until it nearly doubles in size.

4. Collect some glass beads in various sizes and shapes (6–12mm) and push them into the underside of the stack.

5. Remove the beads and backfill the holes made by the beads with solid balls of clay made from the original colors.

6. Flip the stack over and gently press around the balls on the slab.

7. Hold the tissue blade nearly parallel to the clay and make several thin slices across the surface of the slab. Set the slices aside.

Making a barrette

8. Using the barrette hardware as a guide, make a paper template of the size barrette as desired. To make the barrette's base, roll out one of the extra conditioned clays to ⅛" thickness. Place the template over the clay and trim roughly to size. Apply the clay slices to the barrette base randomly. When finished, place a piece of waxed paper over the clay and gently roll over the top of the clay to smooth down the cuttings. Trim the barrette to the template.

9. Place the uncured barrette onto the metal barrette blank, cover with foil, and cure. Note: The barrette must be cured on the metal clip in the oven. This insures the proper shape. Let cool.

Lightly sand or buff the edges of the barrette. Glue the clay to the hardware with E-6000 adhesive.

ANOTHER IDEA

Here's an example of a muted color scheme using the mokume gane technique. You could also make an irregular-shaped cabochon.

PROJECT14
Zinnia Pin

Glow-in-the-dark clay is NOT just for kids! It behaves just like other clays, and I use it regularly when creating beads. I like this project because it combines two of my favorite things: zinnias and smiles. See for yourself when you switch off the light!

Finished diameter: 2"

What You'll Need

Polymer Clay
- ½ brick main color clay
- ⅛ brick glow-in-the-dark clay
- ⅛ brick creamy yellow
- Liquid polymer clay

Tools & Supplies
- Scrap paper
- Acrylic roller or pasta machine
- 1¾6" round cutter
- Petal or teardrop cutter (check the cake decorating aisles)
- Knitting needle
- Needle
- Makin's Clay extruder
- Small ball tool
- Dedicated oven
- E-6000 adhesive
- Pin back

1. Condition clays as usual. Roll a ⅛"-thick sheet of main color clay. If using a PM, use the thickest setting and double the thickness. Cut out one round with the 1³⁄₁₆" cutter. Cut out 10 petals with the teardrop cutter.

2. Place the petals halfway along the edge of the circle. They should be touching each other.

3. With a knitting needle, secure the petals by gently pressing the ends into the center of the flower shape.

4. Re-roll the leftover clay into a new sheet a bit thinner than the first sheet (thickest setting on the PM). Cut out seven more petals.

5. Repeat steps 2 and 3 to secure the petals.

Flower's center

7. Put the glow-in-the-dark clay into the extruder. With the single-hole template, extrude about 3". Switch the template to the 5-hole template and extrude another 2". Empty the remaining glow clay and place the creamy yellow clay into the barrel. Extrude 2" of clay, using the single-hole template.

6. Draw petal lines on each petal plus additional strokes with a needle for more detail.

TIP If you don't have an extruder, simply roll out fine strands of clay in both the yellow and glow clays.

8. Cut several segments of the thin and thicker glow clay strands ³⁄₁₆". Cut seven segments of the cream yellow clay about ³⁄₁₆" long. This is for the smiley face. Dab a small amount of liquid clay to the base to secure the strands. Carefully place the yellow smiley face in the center of the flower.

9. Add the thicker glow segments. Use the thinner glow segments to fill in the spaces. To check how the smile is looking, take the pin somewhere dark for a peek. Make corrections, if necessary. Use a small ball tool to impress the ends of the smiley face strands.

Sunflowers always make me smile. This one smiles back! I used a different shape mini-cutter for the petals of this sunflower.

10. When the face is set, add the pin back so that the face will be upright. If the pin back has prongs, set them into the uncured clay.

Cure in a dedicated oven per manufacturer's instructions. Let cool completely. Glue the pin back in place with E-6000 adhesive.

PROJECT 15
Sculptural extruded clay pin

When I first opened my extruder's package, I looked through all of the templates and imagined what I could do with them. When I found the hexagon, right away I thought of the natural hexagonal rock formations in northern Scotland called the Giant's Causeway. This pin was inspired by that special place.

Finished dimension: 1¾x1½"

What You'll Need

Polymer Clay
- ½ brick black
- ⅛ brick tan
- ⅛ brick translucent
- ⅛ brick white
- Small amounts of yellow and gold clay
- Liquid polymer clay

Tools & Supplies
- Tissue blade
- Clay ball tool
- Needle
- Adirondack Alcohol Inks (butterscotch, lettuce, cranberry)
- Water-based wood stain
- White acrylic paint
- Needle tool
- Craft knife
- Acrylic roll or pasta machine
- Makin's Clay extruder
- Textured scrapbook paper
- Armor All or other release agent
- 3M sponge sanding block-fine
- Crafter's Pick: The Ultimate! glue
- Freshwater pearl (preferably flat on one side)
- Pin back
- Dedicated oven

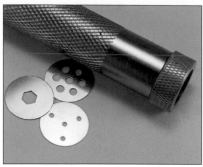

1. Gather the extruder and the hexagon, four-circle, and seven-circle disk templates. Mix the black and tan clays together to create dark, warm gray. Condition as usual. Make pale yellow clay by mixing ⅛ bricks of translucent and white clay with small amounts of yellow and gold clays. Condition as usual.

2. Roll out a sheet of gray clay that's 1¾x1½" and ⅛" thick.

3. Fit the extruder with the four-circle template and load the yellow clay. Extrude 3" of clay. Switch to the seven-circle template. Extrude 3". Cut to ⅛–³⁄₁₆" lengths.

4. Empty the extruder and load with the remaining gray clay. Fix the extruder with the hexagon template. Extrude the clay.

5. Smear some liquid polymer clay onto the clay sheet. Cut hexagons between ⅛" and ³⁄₁₆" long. The pieces should NOT be uniform height. (Turn the hexagon log after each slice of clay. This will help maintain its shape.) Place the hex shapes onto the sheet of clay, beginning at the bottom. Leave a slight gap between the pieces; match up the sides. Continue three-fourths of the way up the sheet. End placement randomly. Gather up the gray scraps and reserve.

6. Begin to place the yellow strands onto the gray clay sheet.

7. With a needle, peck away at one of the hexagons as shown.

8. When finished, trim the pin to the desired shape with the tissue blade.

Dab the flat side of the pearl with some Crafter's Pick: The Ultimate! Glue and place onto the clay, setting gently. Randomly intersperse the fatter strands throughout the rest of the area, being sure to place a few next to the pearl. Take a clay ball tool and gently make little depressions at the top of each strand.

I used a craft knife to pick up and place the pieces.

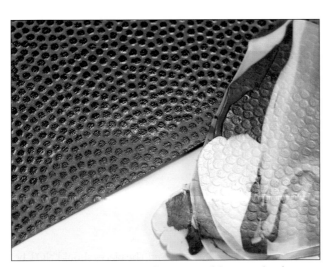

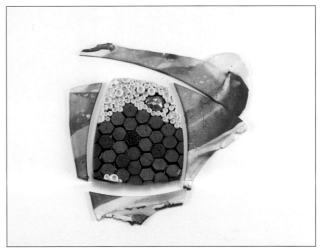

9. Take the yellow and a small amount of the gray clay from the trimmings and roll a thin sheet of clay for the pin backing. It will be mostly yellow and look marbled and striped. Using a piece of textured scrapbook paper, roll the paper over the clay to transfer the texture to the clay's surface.

10. Place the pin on top of the marbled sheet (textured side down) and trim the sheet to fit the pin.

Spray the paper with some Armor All for a release agent.

11. Place the pin backing on the back of the clay. Press gently to set the prongs and remove. Cure in a dedicated oven per manufacturer's instructions. Cool completely.

NOTE You're going to glue this on later, after the pin cures.

12. Tint the yellow strands with a small paintbrush and alcohol inks to add variety to the piece.

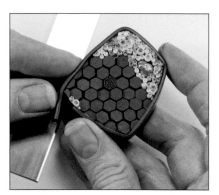

13. Roll out the remaining gray clay into a long strip ¹⁄₁₆" thick (or the thickest setting on the PM) that will wrap the edges of the pin. Cut a straight band of clay around ¼" wide and long enough to surround the pin. Smear the edges of the pin with liquid clay. Starting at the bottom of the pin, place the clay strip so that it is (mostly) flush with the front side of the pin.

14. Continue around the pin and trim to make the ends meet. Heal the seam.

15. Trim the back edges of the pin by sliding the tissue blade around as shown. Cure in a dedicated oven per manufacturer's instructions. Cool completely.

Analogous colors add to the organic feel of the piece. You may also elect to add an additional brown color wash to tone down the hue.

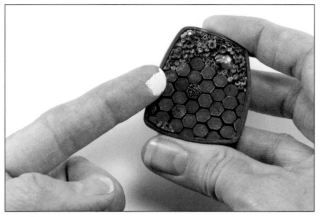

Finishing

16. Take a drop of white paint on your fingertip. Wipe most of it off. Carefully brush your finger over some of the edges of the hex shapes. It's important just to highlight, so make sure that your finger is nearly free of paint.

17. Using a fine sanding block, sand the edges of the pin. Apply glue to the pin back and fit into the prong holes. You're done!

ANOTHER IDEA

I love the sculptural shapes that the clay extruder makes! I applied extruded clay slices to both sides of the pendant, along with paint to highlight the details.

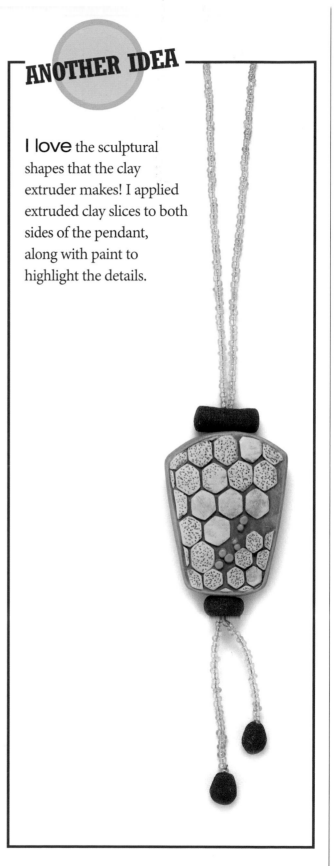

PROJECT 16
Extruded cane pendant

Pendant diameter: 2⅛"

What You'll Need

Polymer Clay
- Assorted colors of polymer clay

Tools & Supplies
- 2" round cookie cutter
- ⅝" round cookie cutter
- ¾" hors d'oeuvre cutter
- Makin's Clay extruder fitted with square disk
- Tissue blade
- Ruler
- Acrylic roller or brayer
- Scrap paper or veggie netting
- Plastic wrap
- Aluminum foil
- Dedicated oven
- Foil
- 400-grit wet/dry sandpaper
- Acrylic floor finish
- Paintbrush
- Cord

This is one of my favorite projects because it is very easy and the results are impressive—even for those who have never played with clay!

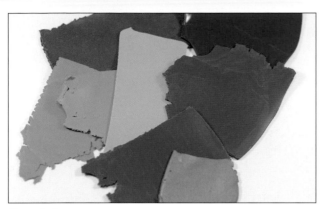

Extruded cane

1. Choose clays that have a variety of colors and contrasts. Condition the clay and roll out to 1/16" thick (or the thickest setting on the PM).

2. Cut out clay circles using a small cutter that measures approximately 3/4" in diameter.

3. Stack the circles (alternating contrasts) until the stack is approximately 5 1/4" long. Insert the clay stack into the extruder barrel.

4. Place the square template into the extruder cap and extrude all of the clay from the barrel. Trim both ends of the extruded clay cane. You will have more than 24".

5. Take the length of extruded clay and cut it in half (12"). Cut in half again (6"). Gently press the lengths together.

TIP If the stack is too fat, roll the stack a little until it fits into the barrel.

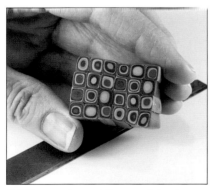

Pendant

7. Condition some solid-colored clay and roll it out to 1/8" thickness. This will be the middle layer. Make several thin, even slices of the extruded cane with a tissue blade. Apply to the solid color layer. Arrange these slices over the middle layer of clay by carefully lining up the cane slice edges.

6. Using a ruler, cut the cane into six 1" pieces yielding a total of 24 1" pieces. Stack the sections 4x6.

TIP Lean directly over the clay when cutting to help make the slice thickness more consistent.

8. Place a piece of waxed paper over the slices and roll it to smooth the edges. Set aside.

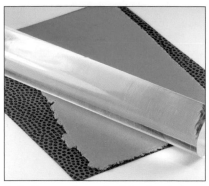

9. Roll out a sheet of solid colored clay in a different color for the backing 1/16" thick (the thickest setting on the PM). To give the backing a texture, turn the clay over and place a piece of textured paper, fabric, or veggie netting over the clay. Gently roll over the fabric or netting to make the impression. Turn the clay over.

10. Place the laminated clay layer over the backing sheet, being careful not to trap air between the layers. Gently roll over the two sheets to adhere them together. Cut a small piece of plastic wrap and place it over the clay. Cut out the pendant using a round 2" cookie cutter. Using plastic wrap when cutting will create a rounded edge.

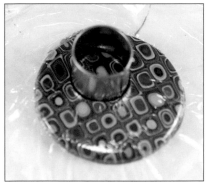

11. With the 5/8" cutter, cut out another hole in the upper half of the circle.

Finishing

12. Remove the plastic. Place on a baking sheet and cover the project with foil. Cure per the clay manufacturer's instructions. Let cool.

13. Sand the edges and surface with 400-grit wet/dry sandpaper, if necessary. If desired, coat the pendant with acrylic floor finish. Apply several coats for a high shine.

Hang the pendant on a color-coordinated cord.

Metallic clays look great extruded! To make this cane, I used gold, fuchsia, ultramarine, green, and violet clays. The top of the pin was textured with a ribbon and cut with a ripple blade. The pearl was set into the clay before curing and reset with glue during finishing.

PROJECT17
Checkerboard cane beads

Checkerboard patterns are fun and easy to add to your technique repertoire. Though simple to do by hand, they provide another great way for you to use your extruder.

Finished length: 7½"

What You'll Need

Polymer Clay
- 1 brick black
- ½ brick white
- ½ brick fuchsia
- ½ brick orange
- ½ brick blue

Tools & Supplies
- Makin's Clay extruder
- Plastic netting (from veggie bags for garlic, lemons)
- Skewers
- Tissue blade
- Acrylic roller or brayer
- Acrylic floor finish
- Pasta machine
- Paintbrush
- 400-grit wet/dry sandpaper
- Dedicated oven

Extrude the clay

1. Fit the clay extruder with the square template and load with the white clay. Turn out the clay, wipe out any clay residue from the barrel, and cap. Reload with the black clay and repeat.

Form the cane

2. Cut each of the square logs into eight equal lengths. Stack the clay to make a 4x4 checkerboard square. Smooth the cane.

3. Roll out a ¹⁄₁₆" (thickest setting on the PM) sheet of orange clay and a ¹⁄₁₆" sheet of fuchsia clay. Change the PM to setting 3 and roll a thinner sheet of ultramarine blue clay. Wrap the clay around the checker board cane in this order: orange, blue, and fuchsia.

 TIP The Makin's Clay Aluminum extruder is durable and comes with 20 disks—great for experimenting with shapes.

4. Smooth the edges after each sheet and trim excess clay. Expel any air bubbles.

5. Smooth and reduce the wrapped cane. To do this, alternate between rolling each side with a brayer and gently twisting the cane from side to side to lengthen it without distorting the pattern. Continue until the cane is four times the original length.

6. Trim the ends and cut the remainder into quarters. Re-stack the checkerboard.

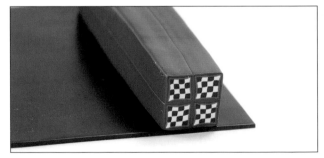

7. Roll out a ¹⁄₁₆" sheet of black clay and wrap it around the checkerboard cane, being careful to trim edges to meet. Lightly roll over the cane with the brayer to adhere the clay.

8. Texture the black clay by placing a piece of netting on the cane, and roll over it, one side at a time, with the brayer. Re-trim the ends.

Make the beads
9. Cut six or seven ¼"-thick slices of the cane (depending on wrist size), turning the cane after every slice. (This helps keep the cane square.) The pattern runs through the beads.

10. Make two holes in each bead: Skewer by poking a needle tool ¼" in from each edge of the beads. Cure and let cool. Wet sand the beads to smooth out the surface and apply two coats of acrylic floor finish to add shine.

TIP String the beads on beading wire with 8mm onyx rounds as spacers for a striking bracelet.

OPTION Omit the black layer from step 7, and skewer the beads on the diagonal. This will give you a contrasting set of beads, perfect to accent a necklace.

ANOTHER IDEA

This pendant combines checkerboard patterns, fractured clay, and textured flower cut-outs.

PROJECT 18
Extruded cane

Finished length: 17½"

What You'll Need

- Several colors of clay, including black and white

Tools & Supplies
- Makin's Clay Extruder
- Makin's Clay Extruder geometric templates
- Tissue blade
- Ripple blade
- Brayer or acrylic roller
- Matboard or Plexiglas square
- Skewers
- Dedicated oven
- Acrylic floor finish

This is a fun and easy way to make complicated-looking designs with polymer clay (these beads remind me of African trade beads). Using your extruder, you'll find that making this cane is much like putting together blocks and shapes like you did as a child. I've also thrown in some more slicing practice with the ripple blade! Experiment and have fun with this one. It's also a good way for you to use up small amounts of leftover clay from other creations.

Preparation

1. Collect several colors of polymer clay (include black and white) and condition as usual. Form the black and white clays each into a 2x1½" block 1" thick. Using the ripple blade, carefully cut several slices of the black and white clay block so that the slices have a consistent thickness to them. Alternately stack the black and white ripple layers.

TIP The best way to cut even slices is to lean right over the clay that you are slicing. This gives you a better view of how straight the blade is going through the clay.

2. Select several geometric shape templates for your extruder. Extrude the colored clay in various shapes.

3. Cut the extruded clay into 2" lengths.

4. Lay the pieces across the ripple stack so that the pattern shows. Continue building the cane by fitting the pieces together until your design is 1½–2" thick.

5. Trim uneven edges and reduce the cane by rolling a brayer or acrylic roller over the stack, turning after each roll.

6. Continue to reduce the cane by gently twisting it until it has doubled in length or is approximately 1¼" wide and 1" tall. Trim the ends and gather up the scrap clay.

7. Make a log from the scrap clay that is ½" in diameter. Cut several thin slices from the cane. Place the slices around the log to cover. Trim the slices so the edges meet evenly.

8. Roll to smooth the edges; this will reduce it slightly. My beads were rolled until they were ⅜" in diameter and 1½" long.

9. Trim the ends of each bead and skewer. Cure per manufacturer's directions in a dedicated oven. Let cool and add two coats of acrylic floor finish for shine. String as desired.

TIP To skewer long beads like these, it's best to twist the skewer back and forth while pushing through the clay.

ANOTHER IDEA

This pattern was created using clays extruded with the triangular template. So simple and so striking!

PROJECT 19
Millefiore flower beads

This cane is a "must-build" for every new polymer clay enthusiast. The name "millefiore" is Italian for "a thousand flowers" and refers to the ancient glass-working technique of building and reducing canes to create complex designs. I'll teach you the Skinner Blend technique for the petals and the center of the flower. The Skinner Blend is a great way to add depth to your clay designs.

Finished length: 18½"

What You'll Need

Polymer Clay
- ½ brick spanish olive
- ¼ brick purple
- ¼ brick white
- ¼ brick maize
- ¼ brick brown

Tools & Supplies
- Acrylic roller or pasta machine
- Tissue blade
- Ruler
- Dedicated clay oven
- Plexiglas or matboard square
- Acrylic floor finish (optional)

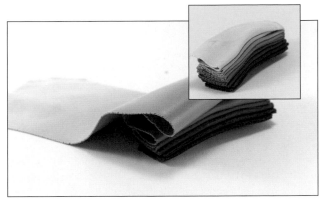

The Skinner blend technique

1. Condition clays. Roll out a 3" square of both plum and white clays. Cut corner-to-corner and separate. Place one plum triangle next to a white triangle, forming a square. Slightly overlap to bind together and fold in half. Roll out to original size. Repeat, folding in the same direction, and roll. Repeat until the colors are well blended.

The petals

2. Roll out the blended clay lengthwise until it's very thin (or use the thinnest setting on the PM), making a long strip of gradually darkening clay. Starting on an end, carefully fold ½" over onto itself and continue accordion-style until the end. Be sure not to trap air between the folds. The result is a rectangular loaf of graduated color!

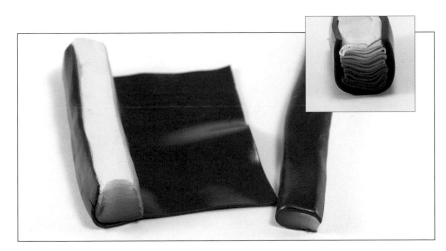

3. Now roll out a sheet of plum clay ¹⁄₁₆" thick that's almost wide enough to wrap around the loaf, leaving the light-colored end exposed. This is the petal. Set aside.

TIP This process may also be done in reverse.

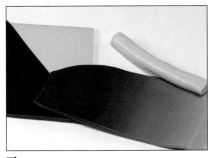

The center

4. Roll out a 3" log of maize-colored clay ¼" in diameter. Set aside. Repeat step 1 with the maize and brown clays.

5. Run the blended clay through the PM lengthwise on the thinnest setting. Trim the ends. Instead of folding the clay, wrap the lighter end of the clay strip onto the maize-colored log that was set aside earlier. This creates a center-graduated cane. Roll to smooth out the seam.

6. Roll to reduce the cane to a log around 25" in length. Trim the ends and cut the log into eight equal sections. Place together, forming little cells. Roll to smooth. Wrap the cane with a layer of maize clay and repeat with another layer of brown clay. This is the flower's center.

Assembling the Flower

7. Take the purple petal loaf and lengthen it to approximately 16" by gently twisting and pulling the loaf to stretch it evenly, occasionally rolling over the sides to smooth. Shape the loaf into petals by rolling over the lighter colored end of the cane to thin it down, forming a triangle with a rounded bottom. Trim the ends. With a ruler, cut the loaf into five equal sections, around 3" long.

TIP

Be sure to check that the petals are well-attached on both ends of the cane. Sometimes a petal doesn't quite get stuck down, and this causes the flower to lose its shape while reducing the cane. The wedges ensure that the petals stay put when reducing the cane. Always make sure that the fit is good when adding filler. If you add too much or too little, the design will end up being distorted.

8. Carefully place the petals around the center to form the flower. Cut wedges of conditioned olive green clay to fit well between the petals.

9. When finished, gently compress the cane to remove air spaces and roll to smooth.

TIP

Turn the cane after every slice to prevent distortion.

10. Wrap the cane with the sheet of green clay and trim clay to fit. Roll the cane to smooth the seam. Reduce the cane to desired flower size by rolling it. Set aside. Roll several balls of olive green clay in graduated sizes.

11. Make several thin slices of the flower cane and apply them evenly over the beads. Roll the beads to smooth them. Skewer and cure in a dedicated clay oven per manufacturer's directions. Let cool. You may opt to leave the beads matte or add shine by applying acrylic floor finish. String as desired.

ANOTHER IDEA

Instead of **making** round beads, apply thin cane slices to a sheet of clay and smooth the surface. Break up the pattern by adding dynamic stripes to the pendant.

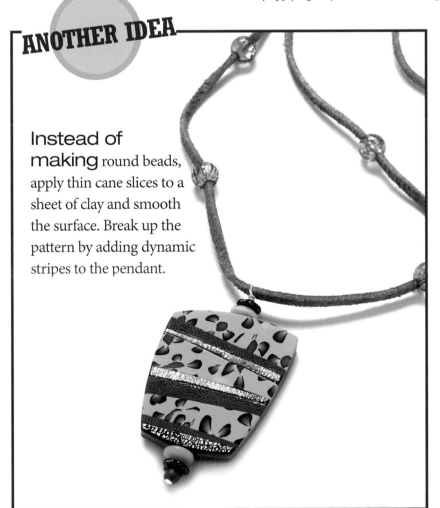

PROJECT20
Modified brain cane

Finished length: 26"

What You'll Need

Polymer Clay
- 1 brick gold
- ¼ brick magenta
- ¼ brick cobalt
- ¼ brick green

Tools & Supplies
- Scrap paper
- Clay extruder (optional)
- Ruler
- Tissue blade
- Matboard or Plexiglas square
- Acrylic roller or pasta machine
- Dedicated oven
- Acrylic floor finish
- Neopaque Black Jacquard
- Artist acrylic paint
- Paintbrush
- Waxed paper

This cane is made by folding clay back and forth in on itself, making it look like a brain! For a traditional brain cane, a very thin sheet of a contrasting color is layered over the main color sheet of clay before folding. The process is easy, and it creates some very fine lines. Here, painting on the clay instead of adding the contrasting layer yields similar results.

1. Condition the clays as usual. Use the Skinner blend technique from Project 19: Roll the clay into a rectangle with ¹⁄₁₆" thickness or the thickest setting on the PM. Trim into a rectangular shape. Cut the clay on a diagonal to make two right triangles. Repeat with the other colored clays. Choose one of the bright colors to be used twice. (I chose magenta.) The color used twice will be the strongest when finished. Roll the gold clay into a longer rectangle the same thickness and cut triangles to match the size of the colored triangles. Pair a gold triangle and a magenta triangle to make a rectangle. Lightly press on the seam to attach the clays to each other. Repeat with the remaining magenta, one blue, and one green.

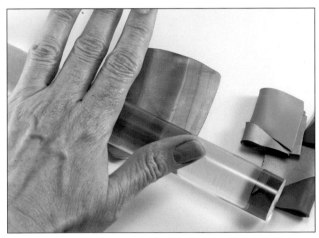

2. Fold the clay rectangle in half vertically. Roll the clay to around the same size it was before it was folded (or, make one pass through the PM on the thickest setting). Repeat in the same direction until the colors are blended.

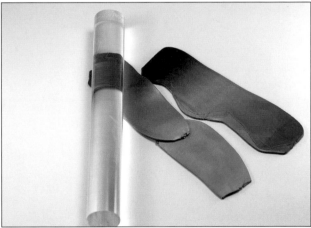

3. Now take one of the pink/gold sheets and one of the other colored sheets and put the gold ends together, slightly overlapping them. Roll the seam smooth. Repeat with the other two sheets of clay.

4. Apply a thin coat of Jacquard black paint. Let dry. Repeat on the other side.

TIP The paint will be sticky so when dry, turn over onto a piece of waxed paper and paint the other side.

5. In the meantime, roll out some gold clay into spaghetti-sized strands (or use a clay extruder). Cut the strands to match the short side of the clay sheets. When the painted sheets are dry, trim the ends of the sheet and wrap it once around one of the gold clay strands. Begin making random size folds and turns with the sheet until it starts to look like a brain pattern, adding other gold strands here and there for interest and volume. When the first sheet finishes, attach the other trimmed sheet and repeat until finished.

6. Lightly press the cane together and gently roll it. Trim the ends.

7. Measure the scrap clay with a ruler. Slice to desired size, and roll into a ball. Make thin slices of the brain cane and cover the scrap clay ball.

8. Roll the covered clay to smooth seams and shape.

9. Skewer the beads, cure, and let cool completely. Apply a coat of acrylic floor finish to the beads. This really brings out the metallic feature of the clay. String as desired.

ANOTHER IDEA

This color scheme includes the addition of a thin sheet of white clay placed over the painted sheet before folding.

PROJECT21
Textured beads

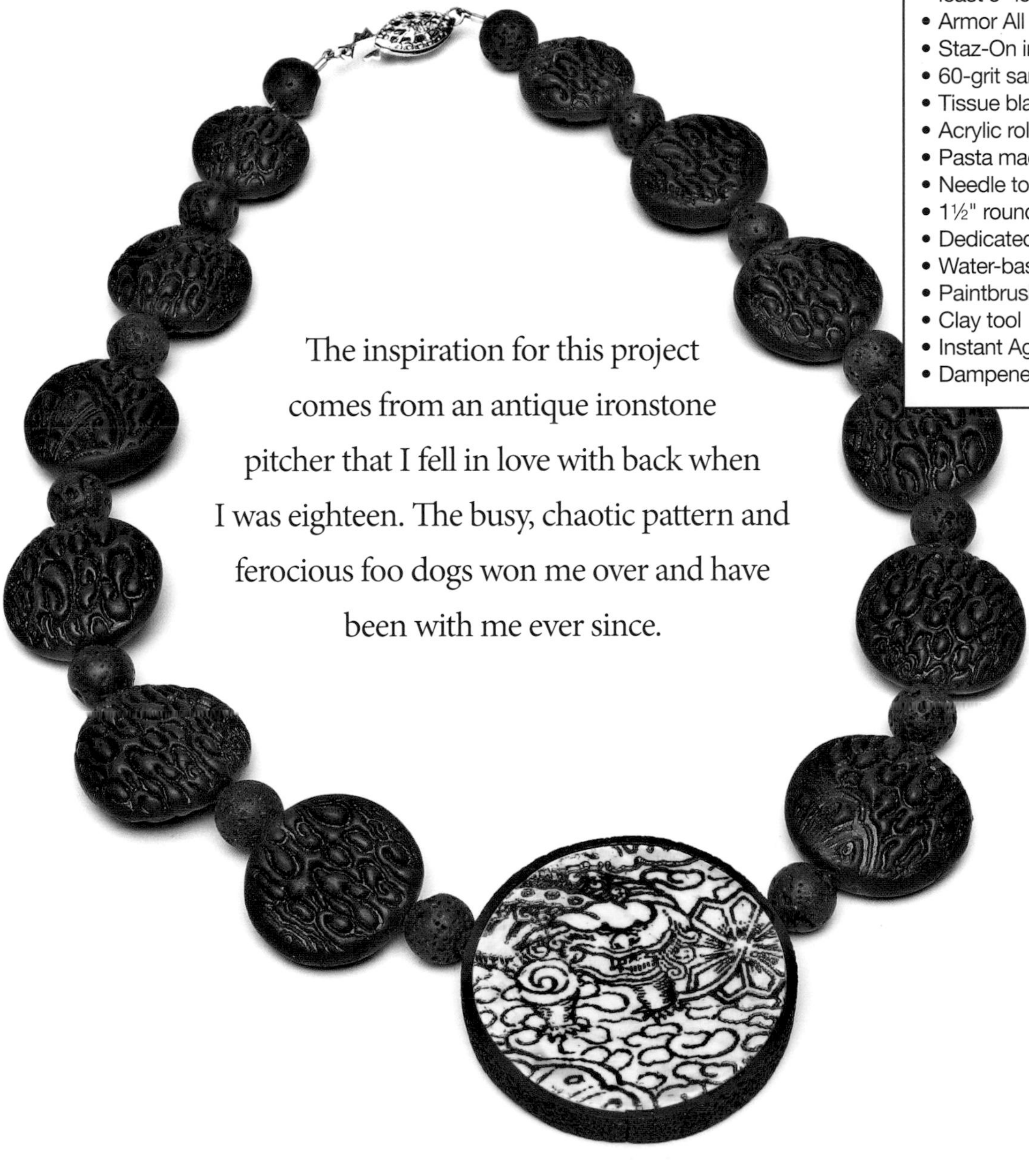

Finished length: 15"

What You'll Need

Polymer Clay
- ⅛ brick white
- ⅛ brick Alizarin crimson
- ½ brick red
- ¼ brick black
- Liquid polymer clay

Tools & Supplies
- Unmounted rubber stamp (at least 3" long)
- Armor All automotive conditioner
- Staz-On ink pad (black)
- 60-grit sandpaper
- Tissue blade
- Acrylic roller or brayer
- Pasta machine
- Needle tool or bead skewer
- 1½" round cookie cutter
- Dedicated oven
- Water-based wood stain (walnut)
- Paintbrush
- Clay tool
- Instant Age acrylic varnish
- Dampened paper towel

The inspiration for this project comes from an antique ironstone pitcher that I fell in love with back when I was eighteen. The busy, chaotic pattern and ferocious foo dogs won me over and have been with me ever since.

1. Condition all clays. Mix the red and crimson clays together. Roll this new mixture into a log ½" in diameter. Using a ruler, mark four different lengths (for example, ½", ⅜", ¼", ⅛"). This creates beads that are graduated in size. (You'll need at least 16 beads to make this necklace.) Roll slices into balls.

2. Lightly spray the flexible stamp with Armor All. Wipe off any excess. (The spray acts as a release agent and helps prevent the clay from sticking to the stamp.) Press a clay ball in between the folded rubber stamp. Be sure to impress the clay to the edges. Repeat with the other clay balls. If you don't like the impression, re-roll and try again.

3. Skewer the beads with a needle tool.

4. Roll out a ¹⁄₁₆" sheet of conditioned white clay. With the 1½" round cookie cutter, cut out a circle.

5. Ink up a desired section of the unmounted rubber stamp and stamp the clay round. Set aside. Clean the stamp.

Cure the red beads and the white stamped pendant round per manufacturer's instructions in a dedicated oven and cool completely.

TIP

Staz-On inks are alcohol inks that work beautifully with polymer clay.

6. Roll out a 2" sheet of red clay ⅛" thick. Cut out a round with the cookie cutter. Place a skewer ¼" down from the top of the round and press. This creates a channel for the beading wire.

7. Smear the back of the cured pendant round with a few drops of liquid polymer clay. This acts as "glue" for the cured clay and the uncured clay. Place the round over the skewered clay and gently press the two together. Cure and let the pendant cool.

8. Roll out a rectangle of black clay at least 7" long, ½" wide, and ⅟₁₆" thick (PM on the thickest setting). Lay a new piece of 60-grit sandpaper over the clay. Gently roll the paper with a brayer or acrylic roller to create the texture.

9. Cut a round from the black clay with the cookie cutter for the pendant's back. Reserve the remaining clay sheet. Smear the back of the pendant round with liquid polymer clay and cover with the textured black round. Match the edges. Cure the pendant per manufacturer's instructions and let cool.

10. Cut a ³⁄₁₆" wide strip from the remaining textured black clay for the finished edge. Apply a small amount of liquid clay around the edges of the pendant. Starting at the bottom, attach a strip of clay so that it is flush with the front side of the round. Work your way around, marking and poking the skewer holes as you go along. Trim where the ends meet at the bottom.

11. "Heal" the clay to mend the seam with a clay tool (you may need to touch up with sandpaper). Carefully trim any excess clay from the back of the pendant. Cure and let cool.

Finishing the beads

12. Apply two thin coats of instant-age varnish to the pendant face and let dry. Coat the stamped red beads with water-based wood stain in walnut. Wipe off the excess stain and let dry. This brings out the stamped design. String as shown on page 79.

ANOTHER IDEA

These earrings are made the same way as the necklace project, only they're skewered from top to bottom.

PROJECT22
Carved beads

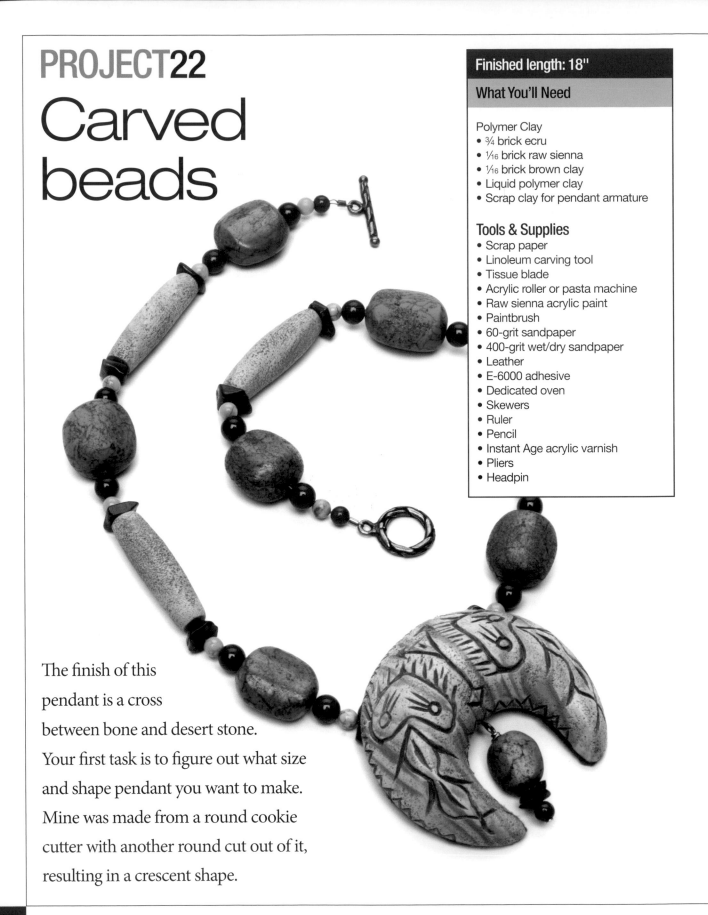

What You'll Need

Polymer Clay
- ¾ brick ecru
- ¹⁄₁₆ brick raw sienna
- ¹⁄₁₆ brick brown clay
- Liquid polymer clay
- Scrap clay for pendant armature

Tools & Supplies
- Scrap paper
- Linoleum carving tool
- Tissue blade
- Acrylic roller or pasta machine
- Raw sienna acrylic paint
- Paintbrush
- 60-grit sandpaper
- 400-grit wet/dry sandpaper
- Leather
- E-6000 adhesive
- Dedicated oven
- Skewers
- Ruler
- Pencil
- Instant Age acrylic varnish
- Pliers
- Headpin

The finish of this pendant is a cross between bone and desert stone. Your first task is to figure out what size and shape pendant you want to make. Mine was made from a round cookie cutter with another round cut out of it, resulting in a crescent shape.

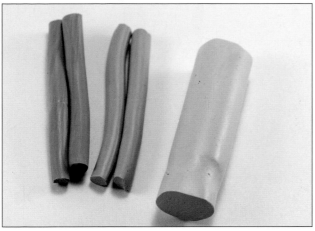

1. Condition all clays. Cut the ecru clay into two pieces, one approximately ½ brick and one approximately ¼ brick. Cut the ¼ brick into two equal pieces. Mix raw sienna with one section and brown with the other. With the remaining ½ brick of ecru, make a log ½" thick in diameter. This will be the base clay. Roll the other two clays into logs twice the length of the base clay. Cut them into halves.

2. Place them along side of the base clay and roll the log.

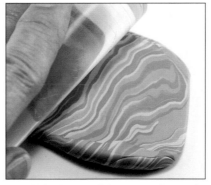

3. Twist, lengthen and roll the log. Fold as shown. Re-roll and repeat twice.

4. Roll the log to ½" diameter. Flatten the log with an acrylic roller. Run the sheet through the PM at the thickest setting. Set aside.

The armature

5. Sculpt the underlying shape, or armature, of the pendant. Use scrap clay to build dimension and when finished, cure per manufacturer's instructions in a dedicated oven.

NOTE If your armature is thick, it will need more time to cure. When cooled, refine the shape to get rid of bumps and imperfections by sanding. Brush on a thin coat of liquid polymer clay to glue the clays together.

ANOTHER IDEA

For this necklace, I made several small blue cabochons, cured them, and carved into them with a linoleum carving tool. To highlight, I rubbed white paint into the carvings.

6. Cut a piece of clay from the sheet large enough to cover the pre-baked armature. Brush on a thin coat of liquid polymer clay, then smooth the sheet of clay over the armature, making sure that there are no air bubbles under the sheet. Trim as necessary.

7. Texture the pendant with sandpaper, if desired. I dabbed a piece of 60-grit sandpaper all over the surface. Cure in a dedicated oven. Let cool completely.

TIP

Remember that once it's been carved, it can't be put back, so make careful marks.

8. Find a pattern or design that will work well on the shape you've created. I found inspiration in the Dover Polynesian image book. Using a pencil, lightly draw the design onto the cured clay.

9. Use the linoleum carving tool and begin to lightly cut out the design.

10. When you've finished carving, paint some raw sienna acrylic paint over the pendant and then wipe off the excess with a dampened paper towel. Take a look. Do you want to add more carvings? I did! Keep going until you're satisfied. Let the paint dry and then wet sand with 400-grit sandpaper. Finish with a coat of Instant Age acrylic varnish.

11. Turn the pendant over. Using a ruler, draw a straight line across the back for the beading wire. Carve it out with the linoleum tool. To add a dangle, I carved a curved line in the clay for a headpin.

Finishing

12. To finish the pendant, cut an 18" piece of beading wire and a headpin for the dangle. Place them into the carved lines.

TIP

Curve the line to secure the headpin, or gravity will eventually let the headpin drop out of the pendant. The curve secures the pin.

13. Smear a layer of E-6000 adhesive to the back and place a piece of leather over it. Let dry and trim leather to fit. The necklace side beads and dangle are polymer turquoise (see Project 6, Faux turquoise). The tube beads are made from the remaining mixed tan clays. Simply roll out a log of the tan clay and slice to the desired length (mine were 1½" long). Skewer and gently roll on each end to create a subtle taper. Texture with sandpaper and cure. Paint with the raw sienna acrylic paint and wipe off excess paint as before. Let dry and string.

PROJECT23
Stamped and inkwashed pendant

This project illustrates how you can use rubber stamps and alcohol inks with polymer clay. In essence, we're color-washing and stamping a small canvas that we'll turn into a wearable note pendant.

Finished length: 3"

What You'll Need

Polymer Clay
- ⅛ brick white
- ⅛ brick scrap clay
- ⅛ brick black
- Liquid polymer clay

Tools & Supplies
- Scrap paper
- Flexible tissue blade
- Clay tool
- Text rubber stamp
- Craft knife
- Staz-On stamp pad (timber)
- Armor All
- Ranger Adirondack Alcohol Inks (in desired colors)
- Paintbrush
- Isopropyl alcohol
- Paint mixing tray
- Bead skewer
- Textured scrapbook paper
- Dedicated oven
- Wire or headpin
- Assorted beads

NOTE I've shown two versions of the pendant to illustrate the different look that's achieved when the stamping and inking steps are done before or after the clay has been cured. The looks are very different. The right pendant was stamped and inked while the clay was uncured or raw. This enabled me to impress the stamp into the clay. It also allows for more blurring of the script. The pendant on the left was cut and cured before stamping and then inks were applied. The result is a bit clearer and more defined. The following directions are for the pre-cured pendant on the left.

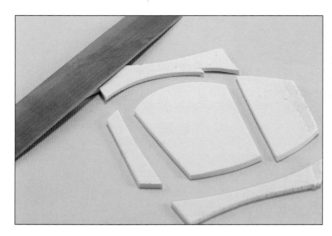

1. Condition all the clays. Roll out a sheet of white clay 2x2" about 1⁄16" thick. Cut into desired pendant shape with a flexible tissue blade. Start with the sides and then cut the top and bottom. Cure in a dedicated oven per manufacturer's instructions and let cool.

TIP Practice cutting with a tissue blade beforehand on some scrap clay.

2. Apply ink to the text stamp, and stamp the white clay. Let dry.

3. To add more interest, I decided to use a light alcohol ink color-wash. This step could have been done before it was stamped, but I wanted an organic, dreamy look. If you prefer a crisper image, simply apply the wash, let dry, and then stamp the text on the clay. Dampen a small paintbrush with some alcohol. Dip the brush tip into a drop of the Ranger alcohol ink and gently color the stamped white clay. Be careful not to work the stamped writing too much because it will be removed. Let dry.

4. Condition the filler/scrap clay and then roll into a sheet 1⁄16" thick. Using the cured pendant as a template, place it on top of the scrap clay sheet and trim off the excess with a craft knife or tissue blade.

5. Remove the pendant and place a skewer vertically over the center of the scrap clay. Gently press the skewer into the clay to make a clear channel for the headpin or wire. Smear a drop or two of liquid clay on the back of the pendant. Place the pendant back over the scrap clay sheet, matching up the edges, re-trimming if necessary. Cure for 10 minutes and let cool.

6. While the pendant is curing, roll out a thin (second-thinnest setting on the PM) sheet of black clay around 3"x 6½" and ¹⁄₁₆" thick. A fun way to add texture is to roll over the clay with a piece of textured scrapbook paper. (Lightly spray some Armor All onto the paper first.) Roll a brayer or roller over the paper and clay. You can also run the paper and clay through the pasta machine. Turn the clay smooth side up.

7. Smear a small amount of liquid clay on the back of the pendant. Place the pendant on the clay. Cut around the pendant and trim the edges flush. Cure as directed and let cool.

8. Cut one long ¼" strip of the black clay to wrap around the pendant. Apply some liquid clay to the edges of the pendant. Starting at the bottom, attach the clay strip flush with the front of the pendant. Clear the hole at the top and continue along the side to the bottom. Trim the strip to make ends meet and mend where they join with a clay tool.

9. Carefully trim the excess strip flush with the back of the pendant with a tissue blade by sliding the blade around the pendant at an extreme angle. Cure as directed and let cool.

10. Finish your pendant with beads and embellishments.

ANOTHER IDEA

These earrings

have a magenta ink wash and black ink script stamp. The edges are wrapped in black.

TIP When adding wrapped edges, begin at the bottom of a piece because it is less visible.

PROJECT24
Shamrock pin

Why wait for Saint Patrick's Day to enjoy this fun pin? Use techniques from previous projects while adding a new one to your list—making cookie cutter canes. This project incorporates three different techniques: stamping, cracked foils, and cookie cutter canes.

Finished length: 2⅛"

What You'll Need

Polymer Clay
- ½ brick cream-colored
- ¾ brick green
- ¼ brick bright green pearl
- ¼ brick black
- ⅛ brick gold
- liquid polymer clay

Tools & Supplies
- Shamrock mini-cookie cutter
- Paper template
- Acrylic roller or pasta machine
- Scrap paper
- Tissue blade
- Clay tool
- Rubber stamp
- Green acrylic paint
- Paintbrush
- Bristle brush
- Instant Age varnish
- Armor All
- Dedicated oven
- 400-grit wet/dry sandpaper
- E-6000 adhesive
- Pin back
- ¼ sheet copper metal foil

Preparation
Condition all clays. Create a paper template of the pin shape.

Shamrock
1. Roll out a slab of green clay ¼" thick and cut six shamrocks using the shamrock mini-cookie cutter. Stack carefully to maintain shape. Smooth edges, if necessary.

2. Roll a log of cream colored clay ¾" in diameter until it is 1½" long. Stand on end. Punch out the center of the cream log with the shamrock cutter. (Brush the cutter with Armor All to help it release easier.)

3. To make the shamrock stem, roll out a small sheet of green clay ¹⁄₁₆" thick. Trim to ¼x1½". Cut through the cream log where the stem will be placed. Take the stacked green shamrocks, plus the stem, and place inside the cut-out cream log. Gently close the cream clay around the shamrock.

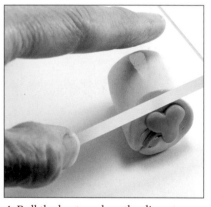
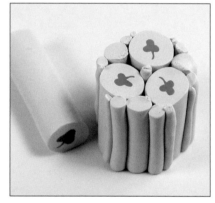

4. Roll the log to reduce the diameter to ⅜".

5. Cut the cane into thirds and re-stack together, with stems pointing toward the center. With the remaining cream clay, roll out a log of filler clay and cut into 1½" lengths. Fill in as shown. This helps to maintain spacing and prevent distortions in the cane design. Gently press together and roll to smooth.

6. Roll out a ¹⁄₁₆" (thickest setting on the PM) thick sheet of remaining cream clay. Make several thin slices of the shamrock cane and randomly place the slices over the cream sheet. Smooth slices down with an acrylic roller and run through the pasta machine on the thickest setting. Turn the thickness down one click and pass through again. Set the sheet aside.

Option Add texture by stippling the shamrock sheet with a bristle brush.

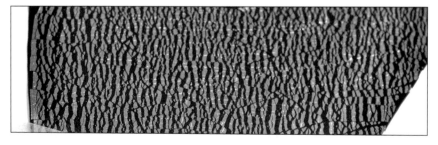

The Fractured Metal Clay Strip
7. Roll out the black clay to ⅛" thickness. Apply the copper leaf to the clay and smooth it down. Roll over the leaf with the acrylic roller to secure it and then through the PM on the thickest setting. Turn the thickness dial down one click and repeat until satisfied. Cut a thin strip 2½x⅛". Set the strip aside and reserve the rest of the fractured clay sheet for another project.

8. Next, roll out a 3x2" sheet of bright green pearl clay on the PM's second-thickest setting. Take a rubber stamp and press it into the sheet of clay.

9. Lay a paper template over the green clay and cut around it using a tissue blade or craft knife. Repeat with the shamrock/cream sheet. Begin to think about the placement of the copper foil strip.

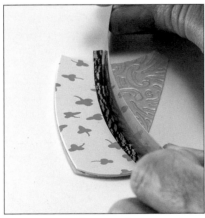

Gently roll the slices down to secure and run the clay through the pasta machine on the thickest setting. Continue to thin the sheet lengthwise one click at a time until the third thinnest setting is reached. Trim the ends.

10. Determine how much shamrock you want on your pin. To do this, lightly lay the shamrock clay over the green clay, position the copper strip, and slice through both layers on each side of the strip. Carefully separate the sheets from the green.

11. Roll out a ¹⁄₁₆"-thick sheet of green clay that slightly exceeds the size of the pin. Place the cut pieces on top and trim as necessary. Gently roll over the stacked clays to bond and expel air, being careful of the textures. Set the pin back. Cure and cool as directed.

The striped edging

12. To make the striped edging, gather the remaining green clay and divide in half. Mix the gold clay with an equal amount of green to make green-gold. Roll into a sheet on the second-thickest setting of the PM. Roll out the remaining green clay. Trim the sheets to the same size and make a striped slab. Gather and mix together all of the green scraps and roll out a sheet on the third thinnest setting of the PM. Take several thin, even slices of the striped cane and place them over the clay, carefully matching up the edges.

  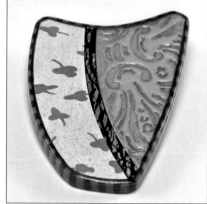

13. Cut a few strips wide enough to cover the side edges of the pin. Smear a few drops of liquid polymer clay on the edges of the pin and wrap the striped clay around the pin, starting at the bottom. Trim the ends and heal the seam with a clay tool. Trim any excess clay from the back. Cure in a dedicated oven as directed and let cool.

Add finishing details
14. Apply green acrylic paint to the impressions left by the rubber stamp. Wipe off the excess paint and let dry.

15. Lightly dry sand the striped edges and the green pearl clay with 400-grit wet/dry sandpaper. Do not sand the foil strip because the leaf will be removed. Apply two or three coats of Instant Age varnish to the pin to bring out the texture. Add some adhesive to the pinback and press it onto the pin.

ANOTHER IDEA

Here's another example of the cookie cutter cane using a star cutter. I paired it with stripes and added a band of textured gold that's been highlighted with a brush of Pearl-Ex gold powder before curing.

Glossary

Acrylic roller—with a non-stick surface, it rolls smooth, even sheets of clay.

Alcohol inks—fast drying, transparent inks. Great for creating watercolor effects.

Armature—a framework used in sculpting or modeling to create a shape.

Beading substrate—a thin, stiff felt used as a cabochon backing for beading.

Bi-cone beads—beads that have a cone shape at both ends.

Brain cane—A cane made by folding sheets of clay back and forth creating a rippled pattern resembling a brain.

Brayer—a handheld rolling tool generally used to apply ink in print making.

Bull's eye cane—a very simple cane made by wrapping a clay sheet around a clay log, creating concentric circles.

Cabochon—domed or convex-shaped clay with a flat bottom.

Cane—several clay logs placed together lengthwise to create a design; when sliced horizontally, the pattern is revealed. Canes can be any shape including round, square, or triangular.

Center-graduated cane—a cane that gradually changes hue or value from the center outward.

Chevron pattern—an alternating diagonal pattern.

Clay glaze—a qick-drying brush-on finish that protects the cured clay.

Conditioning—preparing the clay so that it is workable, smooth and pliable.

Craft knife—a precision cutting blade used to cut clay, trim excess, or create a beveled edge.

Crimp bead—a small metal bead that when crimped (or pinched) holds the stringing wire in place.

Cure—to harden polymer clay by exposure to heat.

Dedicated oven—a non-food use toaster oven or conventional oven.

Dremel drill—a handheld tool that has many useful bits, including drills, buffing felts, and muslins.

Extruder—a tool used to push out different shaped strands of clay.

Flexible tissue blade—a long razor blade used for cutting arcs and curves from sheets of clay.

Foil—extremely thin and delicate foils of metals such as gold, silver, or copper.

Grommets—small metal eyelets sold in the scrapbooking section. Used as an opening.

Headpin—ranges from about 1–3" in length and available in a variety of wire gauges. A headpin looks like a skinny nail and is used to string beads for a link or dangle.

Heal the seam—mending the seam where two sheet of clay meet by rolling or stroking with your fingertip.

Jelly roll cane—a cane made by layering sheets of polymer clay and then rolling them into a spiral.

Linoleum carving tool—a handheld printmaking tool with various interchangeable carving blades.

Liquid polymer clay—polymer clay in liquid form. Used as a "glue" to bond clay to clay. Also for surface application.

Log—a cylinder made from a ball of clay, usually by rolling it between your hand and the work surface.

Marxit tool— a plastic tool marked in increments that can be pressed into the clay for easy and uniform cutting.

Matboard—heavy cardboard originally used to mat pictures in frames.

Matte—dull finish. Not shiny.

Millefiore—means "a thousand flowers" in Italian. Term for glass-making technique in which a flower pattern is repeated many times in the same glass cane and is easily reproduced in a polymer clay cane.

Mokume gane technique—a Japanese metalworking technique that produces random, organic surface patterns resembling burled wood. This technique is easily adapted to polymer clay.

Needle tool—a hand-tool with a needle on one end.

Pearl Ex—very fine mica powder sold in art/craft stores. Adds luster to clay.

Reduce—making a cane smaller or longer by rolling.

Ripple blade—a very thin blade that is used to cut ripple slices of clay.

Sanding block—a sponge that is covered with a flexible sandpaper. Found in woodworking sections of stores.

Skewer—a pointed, thin rod used to hold beads during the curing process.

Skinner blend technique—developed by Judith Skinner, this technique allows for two different clays to be blended together to produce a subtle graduation of the two colors.

Spacers—small beads strung between other beads. Design element.

Surgeon's knot—very strong knot similar to a square knot, but with an extra wrap at the beginning.

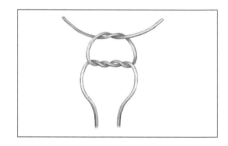

Tissue blade—a very thin razor originally used by pathologists when looking at tissue samples. Essential for making thin, clean cuts in clay.

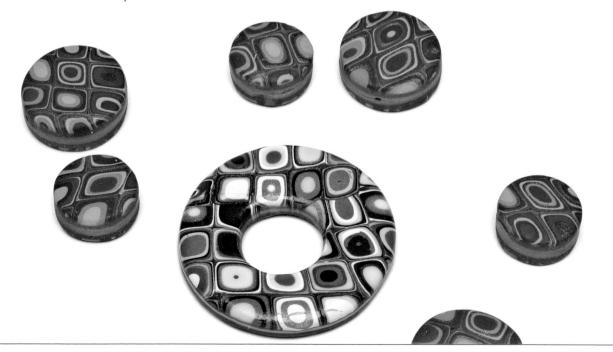

From the author

As long as I can remember, I've always wanted to make things. My first little creations were Q-tip and toilet paper dolls. My dad still talks about those little beauties. When I reached high school, I was very fortunate to have an eccentric but serious art teacher named Miss Hogan. She not only taught us the fundamentals of design, she also passed along a profound respect for making art. You had to have passion and skill to succeed in her classes! During my college years, I used my creative energies on communication and marketing projects (my areas of study), although I did spend my freshman year as a theater major (oops!). After college, I managed a sales territory which drew upon a different set of creative energies but all the while, I continued to make art.

When my husband, Dave, and I started our family, we quickly realized that our priorities had changed forever. The birth of our second son coincided with a job offer for Dave in faraway Ohio (we lived in Rhode Island), so we packed our bags and made a new life in a new area. I was a full-time mother, and for the first time in ages, I had the time to live creatively, squeaked in between naps and at after bedtimes, of course.

My introduction to polymer clay came while watching the tail-end of an HGTV segment featuring the work of polymer artists Ford and Forlano. They were making some incredible polymer clay-covered eggs, and I was smitten. I managed to find a few bricks of clay locally. I bought primary colors and set to work. I had no tools whatsoever. Plus, the clay was so hard that Dave and I had to sit for an hour with the packaged clay tucked into our armpits to make it workable. My first canes were absolutely horrible. Not only were the colors hideous, I had burned the covered eggs in the oven as well. I don't know why I continued, but I did. Maybe I sensed that there were a ton of creative possibilities in the clay, if I just stuck with it. So I did, and soon I was making necklaces. The beads were still kind of ugly, but when I put them together with spacers on a cord, they looked okay. Pretty good, in fact. My favorite necklace from that early phase has teething marks from my younger son who chewed on it while I carried him around!

I've learned so much by working with clay—and not just clay techniques. Since I began, I've set up my own studio, developed an online gallery (come visit me at www.millori.com), done art shows in many states, taught classes, published a bunch of magazine articles, learned to use a real camera, and now I have a book of projects to share with my fellow art-travelers. The great thing is, there's always more to learn!

Acknowledgments

First, I want to thank God for the gift of creativity. His inspiration is both beautiful and endless. I'm also grateful to my parents and grandparents for instilling a strong work ethic in me. Hard work really does pay off.

I love projects. In fact, there's a pretty constant parade of them in my world. I couldn't do them though without my best friend and husband, Dave. He always supports everything I do, and lots of the time, he gets pulled in to make it happen. This book is no different. He has read over every paragraph in every project, checked for subject/verb agreement, and flagged phrasing that needed to be changed. He has encouraged me, taken some photos, and ensured me the space and peace needed to get the work done. Our two great boys, Mason and Haddon, have given up many hot meals in exchange for quick sandwiches without complaining and were kind to their distracted mother. I love my family of good sports, and I am very thankful for them.

I also want to thank my editor, Karin Van Voorhees, for her friendly expertise. I've never worked with a book editor before, and she put me right at ease. I'll never forget the relief I felt when I sent off the first flash drive loaded with content for her to review. She confidently took the work and did her thing. Now that I've seen the book's look and layout, I have to say, "Karin, your work and your team's work have taken my breath away."

Finally, to Kalmbach Publishing Co. and Mary Wohlgemuth, thanks for the tremendous opportunity to bring my ideas to life. I have learned so much in the process. It's been a blessing.

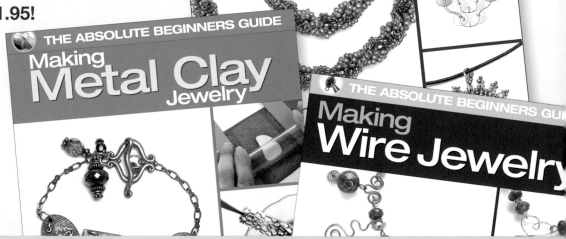